SHAKESPEARE'S SONNETS

SHAKESPEARE'S SONNETS

AND

A LOVER'S COMPLAINT

Edited, with an Introduction, by

STANLEY WELLS

OXFORD
AT THE CLARENDON PRESS

Oxford University Press, Walton Street, Oxford OX2 6DP

Oxford New York Toronto
Delhi Bombay Calcutta Madras Karachi
Kuala Lumpur Singapore Hong Kong Tokyo
Nairobi Dar es Salaam Cape Town
Melbourne Auckland

and associated companies in
Beirut Berlin Ibadan Nicosia

Oxford is a trade mark of Oxford University Press

Published in the United States by
Oxford University Press, New York

© Oxford University Press 1985

First published 1985
Reprinted 1985

The text of this edition is that prepared for the forthcoming
Complete Oxford Shakespeare

British Library Cataloguing in Publication Data

Shakespeare, William
Shakespeare's sonnets ; and, A lover's complaint.
I. Title   II. Wells, Stanley, 1930-
III. Shakespeare, William. [Sonnets] Shakespeare's
sonnets IV. Shakespeare, William. A lover's
complaint
821'.3   PR2848

ISBN 0 19 812946 7

Library of Congress Cataloging in Publication Data

Shakespeare, William, 1564-1616.
Shakespeare's Sonnets.
1. Sonnets, English. I. Wells, Stanley W.,
1930-   . II. Shakespeare, William, 1564-1616.
Spurious and doubtful works. A lover's complaint. 1985.
III. Title. IV. Title: Sonnets. V. Title: Lover's
complaint.
PR2848.A2W45   1985   821'.3   85 11578

ISBN 0 19 812946 7

Printed in Great Britain
at the University Printing House, Oxford
by David Stanford
Printer to the University

CONTENTS

INTRODUCTION

In Shakespeare's comedy *The Merry Wives of Windsor*, the bashful Abraham Slender, urged by his elders to woo 'sweet Anne Page', wishes he could turn to literature for relief from his inarticulacy : 'I had rather than forty shillings I had my Book of Songs and Sonnets here.' Since Slender's time, many another young lover has turned to Shakespeare's own sonnets for help in his courtship, whether to articulate his feelings for the one he loves or to console himself by reading about someone else's amorous problems.

But Shakespeare's sonnets have spoken not only to young persons in love for the first time but to men and women fully experienced in the ways of love. Though Shakespeare wrote, probably, at a time when sonnet sequences addressed to conventionally beautiful and marble-hearted women were the height of fashion, the situations lying behind his own sonnets are not the conventional stuff of romance. The first seventeen urge the poet's handsome young friend to marry. After that we learn, usually obliquely, that the friend makes the poet jealous by being friendly with another poet, that he is seduced by the poet's mistress, and that the mistress, far from being marble-hearted, is 'the bay where all men ride' (137). The most idealistic, lyrical sonnets celebrating lovers' mutuality and exulting in love's illusory triumph over time are written by one man about another. (Number 20 implies that their relationship is not sexual.) The sonnets clearly addressed to a woman revile her for cruelty and infidelity, speak ill of her appearance, and explore a self-disgusted emotional and physical entanglement in language of, at times, gross sexuality.

Shakespeare's sonnets can be seen, then, as both an endorsement of a convention and a fierce reaction against it. The spectacular but brief modishness of the English sonnet sequence can be precisely dated. Sir Philip Sidney's sequence, *Astrophil and Stella*, written around 1582, appeared in print in 1591. During the following six years some twenty sequences were published, some by poets who are still remembered, such as Samuel Daniel, Michael Drayton, and Edmund Spenser. Most of them are about secular love ; a few are on religious themes. Shakespeare's plays of this period reflect the fashion. In the comedy of *Love's Labour's Lost* the writing of sonnets is seen as a laughable symptom of love : the King of Navarre and his lords pen poems to their ladies, and are mocked for doing so. In the tragedy of *Romeo and Juliet*, both speeches of the Chorus and the lovers' first, rapt conversation are in sonnet form.

It is probably during this same period that Shakespeare

wrote most of his private sonnets, but they appear to have been slow to reach print. None had appeared by 1598, when a minor writer, Francis Meres, declared that 'the sweet, witty soul of Ovid lives in mellifluous and honey-tongued Shakespeare, witness his *Venus and Adonis*, his *Lucrece*, his sugared sonnets among his private friends, etc. . . .'. Poems often circulated in manuscript, sometimes reaching print against their author's will. We offer (pp. 185-189) alternative versions of two of Shakespeare's sonnets deriving from seventeenth-century manuscript collections, and of two others which appeared in an unauthorized volume, *The Passionate Pilgrim*, attributed to Shakespeare but including a number of poems that he certainly did not write. His collected sonnets did not appear for another ten years, and then under somewhat mysterious circumstances.

The two narrative poems — *Venus and Adonis* and *The Rape of Lucrece* — mentioned by Meres had been published in 1593 and 1594 respectively, each with a dedication over Shakespeare's name to the Earl of Southampton. When the Sonnets appeared, in 1609, it was with a dedication by the publisher, Thomas Thorpe, not by the author. The wording of the title-page, *Shakespeare's Sonnets. Never Before Imprinted*, implies that the poems are not new, and suggests, too, that their publication has been eagerly awaited. We must assume that Shakespeare himself was not responsible for it; we can only speculate why. The most obvious explanation is that he regarded the sonnets as peculiarly personal poems, written for himself and, perhaps, 'his private friends', rather than as a professional task. Such an explanation implies that these poems are what they appear to be: essentially autobiographical documents, reflecting the poet's own many-faceted experience. Supporting this is the fact that the poems do not present an ordered, coherent series of events and emotions such as might be expected for a sequence written either fictionally or as a fully public working out of private preoccupations. If the poems are autobiographical in origin then not only Shakespeare but the persons he writes about might have preferred them to remain in manuscript.

'With this key', wrote William Wordsworth of the sonnet form, 'Shakespeare unlocked his heart.' 'If so, the less Shakespeare he', retorted Robert Browning, presumably seeing the poems as a professional performance on the part of a supremely professional writer. It is true that Shakespeare's genius as a dramatic poet enabled him to give intensely felt poetic expression in his plays to no less wide a variety of individual experience than in the sonnets. It is true, too, that some of Shakespeare's sonnets, taken individually, are no more private than, for example, the narrator's comments in his narrative poems. Nor can it be denied that, if Shakespeare's Sonnets do not have the self-evident sequentiality of, for example, the lyrics in Tennyson's *Maud* and *In Memoriam*, nevertheless they either were written, or were later assembled, in a less than totally haphazard order. All the poems clearly addressed to a young man are among the first 126 sonnets; all those clearly addressed to, or concerned with, a woman are among the remaining twenty-eight. After the first group of seventeen, urging a young man to marry in order to perpetuate his beauty, various other subdivisions may be discerned. Sonnets 33 to 35 speak of a rift in the relationship for which the friend is responsible ('No more be grieved at that which thou hast done', 35); in 40 to 42 the poet reluctantly accepts that his friend has become his mistress's lover; 43–5, 47–8, 50–2, and 97–8 imply that the friends are absent from each other; 78 to 86 express jealousy of the friend's relationship with another poet; 87 to 90 express regret that the friend has forsaken the poet; 91 to 96 suggest a relationship resumed in spite of doubts about the beloved's constancy; 117 to 120 are poems of regret and explanation of a lapse in the poet's own fidelity.

Sonnet 126 is irregular in form — a poem of six rhyming couplets — as if to stand as a turning point in the sequence. The poems in the second part are more diverse in mood than their predecessors. They link with the earlier poems in depicting a triangular relationship, epitomized in 144:

> Two loves I have, of comfort and despair,
> Which like two spirits do suggest me still.
> The better angel is a man right fair,
> The worser spirit a woman coloured ill.

The sequence ends with two poems in a different style and tone from all the others: alternative variations on a Latin poem based on an epigram from the Greek Anthology.

So, although many attempts have been made to rearrange the sonnets in an order which might, for one reason or another, seem more logical, there are good reasons to suppose that the order in which they first appeared is not accidental; and no one has hit upon a different order which everyone has agreed to be indisputably better.

The principal puzzle about the Sonnets derives, not from the fact that the volume bears a publisher's, not an author's, dedication, but from the wording of the dedication. The layout and punctuation seem odd, though they may simply result from an attempt at decorativeness. The phrase 'onlie begetter' presumably refers to the inspirer of the sonnets— the young man—though some have interpreted it as an allusion to the procurer of the manuscript. 'Mr. W.H.' provides the biggest puzzle of all. If the manuscript from which

TO.THE.ONLIE.BEGETTER.OF.
THESE.INSVING.SONNETS.
Mr.W.H. ALL.HAPPINESSE.
AND.THAT.ETERNITIE.
PROMISED.

BY.

OVR.EVER-LIVING.POET.

WISHETH.

THE.WELL-WISHING.
ADVENTVRER.IN.
SETTING.
FORTH.

T. T.

Thorpe printed the poems reached him indirectly—not, that is, from Shakespeare himself—how did Thorpe know whom the sonnets were addressed to? And who *is* Mr W.H.? Is he Henry Wriothesley, Earl of Southampton, to whom the narrative poems are dedicated, *The Rape of Lucrece* with special warmth? If so, we must assume that the use of 'Mr' ('Master' in Elizabethan terms) and the reversed initials are part of the attempt at disguise from all but those already in the know that is apparent anyway in the use of initials. Or is 'Mr W.H.' William Herbert, Earl of Pembroke, one of the dedicatees in 1623 (seven years after Shakespeare's death) of the First Folio? Or is he a boy actor called Willie Hughes, as the central character in Oscar Wilde's story *The Portrait of Mr W.H.* supposed? (The name 'Will' is punned on in Sonnets 135-6 and 143, and some have suspected a pun on 'hues' in Number 20.) Or is he someone else, otherwise perhaps unknown to posterity?

Attempts to identify the rival poet and the woman— usually known as the 'Dark Lady', though this is not Shakespeare's phrase—have even less to go on, and have been no more fruitful in their results.

Of course we should like to know the answers to the principal questions raised by the sonnets: do they allude directly to Shakespeare's own experience, and if so, who are the persons involved? If we had the answers, it would affect the way we read them. But it would not affect the greatness of the poems, many of which transcend their ostensible subject matter to become meditations on matters of universal importance: the transience of beauty, and of love; the power of friendship to transform the quality of life; the power of love and art over time; the power and the fragility of love's illusions; the humiliation of emotional and sexual subjection; the capacity of the soul to transcend the body's frailty.

Shakespeare's sonnets include some of the greatest individual love poems in the English language; but there is another, and very different, sense in which the sequence as a whole is a great poem about love, and one which is more challenging to the reader. A continuous reading of the sequence is not easy, partly because the closed form of the sonnet, with the finality of its concluding couplet, does not lead the mind forward, partly because there is no easy narrative sequence, partly because the mood changes so rapidly. Nor is it a comforting experience: poems of confidence are juxtaposed with poems of bitter disillusion, joyful ones with others that speak of self-abasement and, in the later part of the sequence, self-contempt. The single poem which is Shakespeare's Sonnets will never have the popularity of some of its parts, but, in its rapid shifts of mood, its intense exploration of the 'heaven' and the 'hell' of being in love (129), it is far greater than the sum of those parts.

*   *   *

Following the sonnets, Thomas Thorpe prints a narrative poem, 'A Lover's Complaint', with a separate heading and ascription to Shakespeare.

A Louers complaint.

BY

WILLIAM SHAKE-SPEARE.

In spite of this its authenticity has been questioned, but on no good grounds. Certainly it is in some ways unlike Shakespeare's other writings; but he was always ready to experiment. He may have intended it as a companion piece to the sonnets; other poets had included complaints of forsaken lovers with their sonnet sequences. But the relationship of this complaint to the remainder of the volume in which it appears seems, at best, tangential. Like the young man of the sonnets, the man complained of (as in the sonnets, no names are named) is irresistibly attractive; but in deep-dyed duplicity he is more like the Dark Lady. In Shakespeare's plays the character he most resembles is Bertram, in *All's Well that Ends Well*. Perhaps Shakespeare wrote the poem around the same time (*c.*1603-4) as that play, but if so he must have deliberately adopted an old-fashioned style.

Its principal difference from the sonnets lies in its distancing perspectives. A narrator sets the pastoral scene, then fades out. The complaining maiden tells her tale not to him but to an old man who happens to be grazing his cattle nearby; he too is silent once the girl starts to speak. Her complaint contains within itself a second, long complaint — her lover's, ultimately successful, against her hard-heartedness. So the poem is both a narrative and a double complaint (the 'lover' of the title may be either the girl or her lover). The girl is clearly forsaken, but we know little of the circumstances, and neither the listener nor the narrator returns.

'A Lover's Complaint' has its own distinctive tone of voice. As a whole, it adds to our sense of Shakespeare's poetic range, and there is an authentically Shakespearian felicity in the lucid compression of its best lines: 'O father!', the girl exclaims to the cow-herd about her lover's persuasive grief, 'what a hell of witchcraft lies | In the small orb of one particular tear.' But the poem's self-conscious artifice is distant from the immediacy of the sonnets. 'A Lover's Complaint' shows us Shakespeare the Elizabethan poet; the sonnets give us a sense of far more intimate communion with Shakespeare the man — an artist, certainly, but one whose artistry can (as it does in Hamlet's soliloquies) take us into a mind at the very moment that passion and thought interfuse to produce language.

SHAKE-SPEARES

SONNETS.

Neuer before Imprinted.

AT LONDON
By G. Eld for T. T. and are
to be solde by william Aspley.
1609. 24

From fairest creatures we desire increase,
That thereby beauty's rose might never die,
But as the riper should by time decease,
His tender heir might bear his memory;
But thou, contracted to thine own bright eyes,
Feed'st thy light's flame with self-substantial fuel,
Making a famine where abundance lies,
Thyself thy foe, to thy sweet self too cruel.
Thou that art now the world's fresh ornament
And only herald to the gaudy spring
Within thine own bud buriest thy content,
And, tender churl, mak'st waste in niggarding.
    Pity the world, or else this glutton be:
    To eat the world's due, by the grave and thee.

When forty winters shall besiege thy brow
And dig deep trenches in thy beauty's field,
Thy youth's proud livery, so gazed on now,
Will be a tattered weed, of small worth held.
Then being asked where all thy beauty lies,
Where all the treasure of thy lusty days,
To say within thine own deep-sunken eyes
Were an all-eating shame and thriftless praise.
How much more praise deserved thy beauty's use
If thou couldst answer 'This fair child of mine
Shall sum my count, and make my old excuse',
Proving his beauty by succession thine.
    This were to be new made when thou art old,
    And see thy blood warm when thou feel'st it cold.

Look in thy glass, and tell the face thou viewest
Now is the time that face should form another,
Whose fresh repair if now thou not renewest
Thou dost beguile the world, unbless some mother.
For where is she so fair whose uneared womb
Disdains the tillage of thy husbandry?
Or who is he so fond will be the tomb
Of his self-love to stop posterity?
Thou art thy mother's glass, and she in thee
Calls back the lovely April of her prime;
So thou through windows of thine age shalt see,
Despite of wrinkles, this thy golden time.
　　But if thou live remembered not to be,
　　Die single, and thine image dies with thee.

Unthrifty loveliness, why dost thou spend
Upon thyself thy beauty's legacy?
Nature's bequest gives nothing, but doth lend,
And being frank, she lends to those are free.
Then, beauteous niggard, why dost thou abuse
The bounteous largess given thee to give?
Profitless usurer, why dost thou use
So great a sum of sums yet canst not live?
For having traffic with thyself alone,
Thou of thyself thy sweet self dost deceive.
Then how when nature calls thee to be gone:
What acceptable audit canst thou leave?
　　Thy unused beauty must be tombed with thee,
　　Which uséd, lives th'executor to be.

Those hours that with gentle work did frame
The lovely gaze where every eye doth dwell
Will play the tyrants to the very same,
And that unfair which fairly doth excel;
For never-resting time leads summer on
To hideous winter, and confounds him there,
Sap checked with frost, and lusty leaves quite gone,
Beauty o'er-snowed, and bareness everywhere.
Then were not summer's distillation left
A liquid prisoner pent in walls of glass,
Beauty's effect with beauty were bereft,
Nor it nor no remembrance what it was.
    But flowers distilled, though they with winter meet,
    Lose but their show; their substance still lives
        sweet.

Then let not winter's ragged hand deface
In thee thy summer ere thou be distilled.
Make sweet some vial, treasure thou some place
With beauty's treasure ere it be self-killed.
That use is not forbidden usury
Which happies those that pay the willing loan:
That's for thyself to breed another thee,
Or ten times happier, be it ten for one;
Ten times thyself were happier than thou art,
If ten of thine ten times refigured thee.
Then what could death do if thou shouldst depart,
Leaving thee living in posterity?
    Be not self-willed, for thou art much too fair
    To be death's conquest and make worms thine heir.

Lo, in the orient when the gracious light
Lifts up his burning head, each under eye
Doth homage to his new-appearing sight,
Serving with looks his sacred majesty,
And having climbed the steep-up heavenly hill,
Resembling strong youth in his middle age,
Yet mortal looks adore his beauty still,
Attending on his golden pilgrimage.
But when from highmost pitch, with weary car,
Like feeble age he reeleth from the day,
The eyes, 'fore duteous, now converted are
From his low tract, and look another way.
  So thou, thyself outgoing in thy noon,
  Unlooked on diest unless thou get a son.

Music to hear, why hear'st thou music sadly?
Sweets with sweets war not, joy delights in joy.
Why lov'st thou that which thou receiv'st not gladly,
Or else receiv'st with pleasure thine annoy?
If the true concord of well-tunèd sounds
By unions married do offend thine ear,
They do but sweetly chide thee, who confounds
In singleness the parts that thou shouldst bear.
Mark how one string, sweet husband to another,
Strikes each in each by mutual ordering,
Resembling sire and child and happy mother,
Who all in one one pleasing note do sing;
    Whose speechless song, being many, seeming one,
    Sings this to thee: 'Thou single wilt prove none.'

Is it for fear to wet a widow's eye
That thou consum'st thyself in single life?
Ah, if thou issueless shalt hap to die,
The world will wail thee like a makeless wife.
The world will be thy widow, and still weep
That thou no form of thee hast left behind,
When every private widow well may keep
By children's eyes her husband's shape in mind.
Look what an unthrift in the world doth spend
Shifts but his place, for still the world enjoys it;
But beauty's waste hath in the world an end,
And kept unused, the user so destroys it.
    No love toward others in that bosom sits
    That on himself such murd'rous shame commits.

For shame deny that thou bear'st love to any,
Who for thyself art so unprovident.
Grant, if thou wilt, thou art beloved of many,
But that thou none lov'st is most evident;
For thou art so possessed with murd'rous hate
That 'gainst thyself thou stick'st not to conspire,
Seeking that beauteous roof to ruinate
Which to repair should be thy chief desire.
O, change thy thought, that I may change my mind!
Shall hate be fairer lodged than gentle love?
Be as thy presence is, gracious and kind,
Or to thyself at least kind-hearted prove.
   Make thee another self for love of me,
   That beauty still may live in thine or thee.

As fast as thou shalt wane, so fast thou grow'st
In one of thine from that which thou departest,
And that fresh blood which youngly thou bestow'st
Thou mayst call thine when thou from youth
    convertest.
Herein lives wisdom, beauty, and increase;
Without this, folly, age, and cold decay.
If all were minded so, the times should cease,
And threescore year would make the world away.
Let those whom nature hath not made for store,
Harsh, featureless, and rude, barrenly perish.
Look whom she best endowed she gave the more,
Which bounteous gift thou shouldst in bounty cherish.
    She carved thee for her seal, and meant thereby
    Thou shouldst print more, not let that copy die.

When I do count the clock that tells the time,
And see the brave day sunk in hideous night;
When I behold the violet past prime,
And sable curls ensilvered o'er with white;
When lofty trees I see barren of leaves,
Which erst from heat did canopy the herd,
And summer's green all girded up in sheaves
Borne on the bier with white and bristly beard:
Then of thy beauty do I question make
That thou among the wastes of time must go,
Since sweets and beauties do themselves forsake,
And die as fast as they see others grow;
    And nothing 'gainst time's scythe can make defence
    Save breed to brave him when he takes thee hence.

O that you were yourself! But, love, you are
No longer yours than you yourself here live.
Against this coming end you should prepare,
And your sweet semblance to some other give.
So should that beauty which you hold in lease
Find no determination; then you were
Yourself again after your self's decease,
When your sweet issue your sweet form should bear.
Who lets so fair a house fall to decay,
Which husbandry in honour might uphold
Against the stormy gusts of winter's day,
And barren rage of death's eternal cold?
 O, none but unthrifts, dear my love, you know.
 You had a father; let your son say so.

Not from the stars do I my judgement pluck,
And yet methinks I have astronomy;
But not to tell of good or evil luck,
Of plagues, of dearths, or seasons' quality.
Nor can I fortune to brief minutes tell,
'Pointing to each his thunder, rain, and wind,
Or say with princes if it shall go well
By oft predict that I in heaven find;
But from thine eyes my knowledge I derive,
And, constant stars, in them I read such art
As truth and beauty shall together thrive
If from thyself to store thou wouldst convert
   Or else of thee this I prognosticate:
   Thy end is truth's and beauty's doom and date.

When I consider every thing that grows
Holds in perfection but a little moment,
That this huge stage presenteth naught but shows
Whereon the stars in secret influence comment;
When I perceive that men as plants increase,
Cheerèd and checked even by the selfsame sky;
Vaunt in their youthful sap, at height decrease,
And wear their brave state out of memory:
Then the conceit of this inconstant stay
Sets you most rich in youth before my sight,
Where wasteful time debateth with decay
To change your day of youth to sullied night;
    And all in war with time for love of you,
    As he takes from you, I engraft you new.

But wherefore do not you a mightier way
Make war upon this bloody tyrant, time,
And fortify yourself in your decay
With means more blessèd than my barren rhyme?
Now stand you on the top of happy hours,
And many maiden gardens yet unset
With virtuous wish would bear your living flowers,
Much liker than your painted counterfeit.
So should the lines of life that life repair
Which this time's pencil or my pupil pen
Neither in inward worth nor outward fair
Can make you live yourself in eyes of men.
    To give away yourself keeps yourself still,
    And you must live drawn by your own sweet skill.

Who will believe my verse in time to come
If it were filled with your most high deserts?—
Though yet, heaven knows, it is but as a tomb
Which hides your life, and shows not half your parts.
If I could write the beauty of your eyes
And in fresh numbers number all your graces,
The age to come would say 'This poet lies;
Such heavenly touches ne'er touched earthly faces.'
So should my papers, yellowed with their age,
Be scorned, like old men of less truth than tongue,
And your true rights be termed a poet's rage
And stretchèd metre of an antique song.
  But were some child of yours alive that time,
  You should live twice: in it, and in my rhyme.

Shall I compare thee to a summer's day?
Thou art more lovely and more temperate.
Rough winds do shake the darling buds of May,
And summer's lease hath all too short a date.
Sometime too hot the eye of heaven shines,
And often is his gold complexion dimmed,
And every fair from fair some time declines,
By chance or nature's changing course untrimmed;
But thy eternal summer shall not fade
Nor lose possession of that fair thou ow'st,
Nor shall death brag thou wander'st in his shade
When in eternal lines to time thou grow'st.
  So long as men can breathe or eyes can see,
  So long lives this, and this gives life to thee.

Devouring time, blunt thou the lion's paws,
And make the earth devour her own sweet brood;
Pluck the keen teeth from the fierce tiger's jaws,
And burn the long-lived phoenix in her blood.
Make glad and sorry seasons as thou fleet'st,
And do whate'er thou wilt, swift-footed time,
To the wide world and all her fading sweets.
But I forbid thee one most heinous crime:
O, carve not with thy hours my love's fair brow,
Nor draw no lines there with thine antique pen.
Him in thy course untainted do allow
For beauty's pattern to succeeding men.
    Yet do thy worst, old time; despite thy wrong
    My love shall in my verse ever live young.

A woman's face with nature's own hand painted
Hast thou, the master-mistress of my passion;
A woman's gentle heart, but not acquainted
With shifting change as is false women's fashion;
An eye more bright than theirs, less false in rolling,
Gilding the object whereupon it gazeth;
A man in hue, all hues in his controlling,
Which steals men's eyes and women's souls amazeth.
And for a woman wert thou first created,
Till nature as she wrought thee fell a-doting,
And by addition me of thee defeated
By adding one thing to my purpose nothing.
    But since she pricked thee out for women's
        pleasure,
    Mine be thy love and thy love's use their treasure.

So is it not with me as with that muse
Stirred by a painted beauty to his verse,
Who heaven itself for ornament doth use,
And every fair with his fair doth rehearse,
Making a couplement of proud compare
With sun and moon, with earth, and sea's rich gems,
With April's first-born flowers, and all things rare
That heaven's air in this huge rondure hems.
O let me, true in love, but truly write,
And then believe me my love is as fair
As any mother's child, though not so bright
As those gold candles fixed in heaven's air.
   Let them say more that like of hearsay well;
   I will not praise that purpose not to sell.

My glass shall not persuade me I am old
So long as youth and thou are of one date;
But when in thee time's furrows I behold,
Then look I death my days should expiate.
For all that beauty that doth cover thee
Is but the seemly raiment of my heart,
Which in thy breast doth live, as thine in me;
How can I then be elder than thou art?
O therefore, love, be of thyself so wary
As I, not for myself, but for thee will,
Bearing thy heart, which I will keep so chary
As tender nurse her babe from faring ill.
    Presume not on thy heart when mine is slain:
    Thou gav'st me thine not to give back again.

As an unperfect actor on the stage
Who with his fear is put besides his part,
Or some fierce thing replete with too much rage
Whose strength's abundance weakens his own heart,
So I, for fear of trust, forget to say
The perfect ceremony of love's rite,
And in mine own love's strength seem to decay,
O'ercharged with burden of mine own love's might.
O let my books be then the eloquence
And dumb presagers of my speaking breast,
Who plead for love, and look for recompense
More than that tongue that more hath more
      expressed.
   O learn to read what silent love hath writ;
   To hear with eyes belongs to love's fine wit.

Mine eye hath played the painter, and hath steeled
Thy beauty's form in table of my heart.
My body is the frame wherein 'tis held,
And perspective it is best painter's art;
For through the painter must you see his skill
To find where your true image pictured lies,
Which in my bosom's shop is hanging still,
That hath his windows glazèd with thine eyes.
Now see what good turns eyes for eyes have done:
Mine eyes have drawn thy shape, and thine for me
Are windows to my breast, wherethrough the sun
Delights to peep, to gaze therein on thee.
    Yet eyes this cunning want to grace their art:
    They draw but what they see, know not the heart.

Let those who are in favour with their stars
Of public honour and proud titles boast,
Whilst I, whom fortune of such triumph bars,
Unlooked-for joy in that I honour most.
Great princes' favourites their fair leaves spread
But as the marigold at the sun's eye,
And in themselves their pride lies burièd,
For at a frown they in their glory die.
The painful warrior famousèd for might,
After a thousand victories once foiled
Is from the book of honour razèd quite,
And all the rest forgot for which he toiled.
   Then happy I, that love and am beloved
   Where I may not remove nor be removed.

Lord of my love, to whom in vassalage
Thy merit hath my duty strongly knit,
To thee I send this written embassage
To witness duty, not to show my wit;
Duty so great which wit so poor as mine
May make seem bare in wanting words to show it,
But that I hope some good conceit of thine
In thy soul's thought, all naked, will bestow it,
Till whatsoever star that guides my moving
Points on me graciously with fair aspect,
And puts apparel on my tattered loving
To show me worthy of thy sweet respect.
    Then may I dare to boast how I do love thee;
    Till then, not show my head where thou mayst
        prove me.

Weary with toil I haste me to my bed,
The dear repose for limbs with travel tired;
But then begins a journey in my head
To work my mind when body's work's expired;
For then my thoughts, from far where I abide,
Intend a zealous pilgrimage to thee,
And keep my drooping eyelids open wide,
Looking on darkness which the blind do see:
Save that my soul's imaginary sight
Presents thy shadow to my sightless view,
Which like a jewel hung in ghastly night
Makes black night beauteous and her old face new.
  Lo, thus by day my limbs, by night my mind,
  For thee, and for myself, no quiet find.

How can I then return in happy plight,
That am debarred the benefit of rest,
When day's oppression is not eased by night,
But day by night and night by day oppressed,
And each, though enemies to either's reign,
Do in consent shake hands to torture me,
The one by toil, the other to complain
How far I toil, still farther off from thee?
I tell the day to please him thou art bright,
And do'st him grace when clouds do blot the heaven;
So flatter I the swart-complexioned night
When sparkling stars twire not thou gild'st the even.
  But day doth daily draw my sorrows longer,
    And night doth nightly make grief's strength seem
      stronger.

When, in disgrace with fortune and men's eyes,
I all alone beweep my outcast state,
And trouble deaf heaven with my bootless cries,
And look upon myself and curse my fate,
Wishing me like to one more rich in hope,
Featured like him, like him with friends possessed,
Desiring this man's art and that man's scope,
With what I most enjoy contented least:
Yet in these thoughts myself almost despising,
Haply I think on thee, and then my state,
Like to the lark at break of day arising
From sullen earth, sings hymns at heaven's gate;
    For thy sweet love remembered such wealth brings
    That then I scorn to change my state with kings'.

When to the sessions of sweet silent thought
I summon up remembrance of things past,
I sigh the lack of many a thing I sought,
And with old woes new wail my dear time's waste.
Then can I drown an eye unused to flow
For precious friends hid in death's dateless night,
And weep afresh love's long-since-cancelled woe,
And moan th'expense of many a vanished sight.
Then can I grieve at grievances foregone,
And heavily from woe to woe tell o'er
The sad account of fore-bemoanèd moan,
Which I new pay as if not paid before.
    But if the while I think on thee, dear friend,
    All losses are restored, and sorrows end.

Thy bosom is endearèd with all hearts
Which I by lacking have supposèd dead,
And there reigns love, and all love's loving parts,
And all those friends which I thought burièd.
How many a holy and obsequious tear
Hath dear religious love stol'n from mine eye
As interest of the dead, which now appear
But things removed that hidden in thee lie!
Thou art the grave where buried love doth live,
Hung with the trophies of my lovers gone,
Who all their parts of me to thee did give:
That due of many now is thine alone.
    Their images I loved I view in thee,
    And thou, all they, hast all the all of me.

If thou survive my well-contented day
When that churl death my bones with dust shall
    cover,
And shalt by fortune once more resurvey
These poor rude lines of thy deceasèd lover,
Compare them with the bett'ring of the time,
And though they be outstripped by every pen,
Reserve them for my love, not for their rhyme
Exceeded by the height of happier men.
O then vouchsafe me but this loving thought:
'Had my friend's muse grown with this growing age,
A dearer birth than this his love had brought
To march in ranks of better equipage;
    But since he died, and poets better prove,
    Theirs for their style I'll read, his for his love.'

Full many a glorious morning have I seen
Flatter the mountain tops with sovereign eye,
Kissing with golden face the meadows green,
Gilding pale streams with heavenly alchemy;
Anon permit the basest clouds to ride
With ugly rack on his celestial face,
And from the forlorn world his visage hide,
Stealing unseen to west with this disgrace.
Even so my sun one early morn did shine
With all triumphant splendour on my brow;
But out, alas, he was but one hour mine;
The region cloud hath masked him from me now.
    Yet him for this my love no whit disdaineth:
    Suns of the world may stain when heaven's sun
        staineth.

Why didst thou promise such a beauteous day
And make me travel forth without my cloak,
To let base clouds o'ertake me in my way,
Hiding thy brav'ry in their rotten smoke?
'Tis not enough that through the cloud thou break
To dry the rain on my storm-beaten face,
For no man well of such a salve can speak
That heals the wound and cures not the disgrace.
Nor can thy shame give physic to my grief;
Though thou repent, yet I have still the loss.
Th'offender's sorrow lends but weak relief
To him that bears the strong offence's cross.
    Ah, but those tears are pearl which thy love sheds,
    And they are rich, and ransom all ill deeds.

No more be grieved at that which thou hast done:
Roses have thorns, and silver fountains mud.
Clouds and eclipses stain both moon and sun,
And loathsome canker lives in sweetest bud.
All men make faults, and even I in this,
Authorizing thy trespass with compare,
Myself corrupting salving thy amiss,
Excusing thy sins more than thy sins are;
For to thy sensual fault I bring in sense—
Thy adverse party is thy advocate—
And 'gainst myself a lawful plea commence.
Such civil war is in my love and hate
That I an accessory needs must be
To that sweet thief which sourly robs from me.

Let me confess that we two must be twain
Although our undivided loves are one;
So shall those blots that do with me remain
Without thy help by me be borne alone.
In our two loves there is but one respect,
Though in our lives a separable spite
Which, though it alter not love's sole effect,
Yet doth it steal sweet hours from love's delight.
I may not evermore acknowledge thee
Lest my bewailèd guilt should do thee shame,
Nor thou with public kindness honour me
Unless thou take that honour from thy name.
    But do not so. I love thee in such sort
    As, thou being mine, mine is thy good report.

As a decrepit father takes delight
To see his active child do deeds of youth,
So I, made lame by fortune's dearest spite,
Take all my comfort of thy worth and truth;
For whether beauty, birth, or wealth, or wit,
Or any of these all, or all, or more,
Entitled in thy parts do crownèd sit,
I make my love engrafted to this store.
So then I am not lame, poor, nor despised,
Whilst that this shadow doth such substance give
That I in thy abundance am sufficed
And by a part of all thy glory live.
　　Look what is best, that best I wish in thee;
　　This wish I have, then ten times happy me.

How can my muse want subject to invent
While thou dost breathe, that pour'st into my verse
Thine own sweet argument, too excellent
For every vulgar paper to rehearse?
O, give thyself the thanks if aught in me
Worthy perusal stand against thy sight;
For who's so dumb that cannot write to thee,
When thou thyself dost give invention light?
Be thou the tenth muse, ten times more in worth
Than those old nine which rhymers invocate,
And he that calls on thee, let him bring forth
Eternal numbers to outlive long date.
    If my slight muse do please these curious days,
      The pain be mine, but thine shall be the praise.

O, how thy worth with manners may I sing
When thou art all the better part of me?
What can mine own praise to mine own self bring,
And what is't but mine own when I praise thee?
Even for this let us divided live,
And our dear love lose name of single one,
That by this separation I may give
That due to thee which thou deserv'st alone.
O absence, what a torment wouldst thou prove
Were it not thy sour leisure gave sweet leave
To entertain the time with thoughts of love,
Which time and thoughts so sweetly doth deceive,
   And that thou teachest how to make one twain
   By praising him here who doth hence remain!

Take all my loves, my love, yea, take them all:
What hast thou then more than thou hadst before?
No love, my love, that thou mayst true love call—
All mine was thine before thou hadst this more.
Then if for my love thou my love receivest,
I cannot blame thee for my love thou usest;
But yet be blamed if thou this self deceivest
By wilful taste of what thyself refusest.
I do forgive thy robb'ry, gentle thief,
Although thou steal thee all my poverty;
And yet love knows it is a greater grief
To bear love's wrong than hate's known injury.
    Lascivious grace, in whom all ill well shows,
    Kill me with spites, yet we must not be foes.

Those pretty wrongs that liberty commits
When I am sometime absent from thy heart
Thy beauty and thy years full well befits,
For still temptation follows where thou art.
Gentle thou art, and therefore to be won;
Beauteous thou art, therefore to be assailed;
And when a woman woos, what woman's son
Will sourly leave her till he have prevailed?
Ay me, but yet thou mightst my seat forbear,
And chide thy beauty and thy straying youth
Who lead thee in their riot even there
Where thou art forced to break a two-fold troth:
    Hers, by thy beauty tempting her to thee,
    Thine, by thy beauty being false to me.

That thou hast her, it is not all my grief,
And yet it may be said I loved her dearly;
That she hath thee is of my wailing chief,
A loss in love that touches me more nearly.
Loving offenders, thus I will excuse ye:
Thou dost love her because thou know'st I love her,
And for my sake even so doth she abuse me,
Suff'ring my friend for my sake to approve her.
If I lose thee, my loss is my love's gain,
And losing her, my friend hath found that loss:
Both find each other, and I lose both twain,
And both for my sake lay on me this cross.
    But here's the joy: my friend and I are one.
    Sweet flattery! Then she loves but me alone.

When most I wink, then do mine eyes best see,
For all the day they view things unrespected;
But when I sleep, in dreams they look on thee,
And, darkly bright, are bright in dark directed.
Then thou, whose shadow shadows doth make bright,
How would thy shadow's form form happy show
To the clear day with thy much clearer light,
When to unseeing eyes thy shade shines so!
How would, I say, mine eyes be blessèd made
By looking on thee in the living day,
When in dead night thy fair imperfect shade
Through heavy sleep on sightless eyes doth stay!
　　All days are nights to see till I see thee,
　　And nights bright days when dreams do show thee
　　　me.

If the dull substance of my flesh were thought,
Injurious distance should not stop my way;
For then, despite of space, I would be brought
From limits far remote where thou dost stay.
No matter then although my foot did stand
Upon the farthest earth removed from thee;
For nimble thought can jump both sea and land
As soon as think the place where he would be.
But ah, thought kills me that I am not thought,
To leap large lengths of miles when thou art gone,
But that, so much of earth and water wrought,
I must attend time's leisure with my moan,
    Receiving naught by elements so slow
    But heavy tears, badges of either's woe.

The other two, slight air and purging fire,
Are both with thee wherever I abide;
The first my thought, the other my desire,
These present-absent with swift motion slide;
For when these quicker elements are gone
In tender embassy of love to thee,
My life, being made of four, with two alone
Sinks down to death, oppressed with melancholy,
Until life's composition be recured
By those swift messengers returned from thee,
Who even but now come back again assured
Of thy fair health, recounting it to me.
   This told, I joy; but then no longer glad,
    I send them back again and straight grow sad.

Mine eye and heart are at a mortal war
How to divide the conquest of thy sight.
Mine eye my heart thy picture's sight would bar,
My heart, mine eye the freedom of that right.
My heart doth plead that thou in him dost lie,
A closet never pierced with crystal eyes;
But the defendant doth that plea deny,
And says in him thy fair appearance lies.
To 'cide this title is empanellèd
A quest of thoughts, all tenants to the heart,
And by their verdict is determinèd
The clear eye's moiety and the dear heart's part,
   As thus: mine eye's due is thy outward part,
   And my heart's right thy inward love of heart.

Betwixt mine eye and heart a league is took,
And each doth good turns now unto the other.
When that mine eye is famished for a look,
Or heart in love with sighs himself doth smother,
With my love's picture then my eye doth feast,
And to the painted banquet bids my heart.
Another time mine eye is my heart's guest
And in his thoughts of love doth share a part.
So either by thy picture or my love,
Thyself away art present still with me;
For thou no farther than my thoughts canst move,
And I am still with them, and they with thee;
  Or if they sleep, thy picture in my sight
  Awakes my heart to heart's and eye's delight.

How careful was I when I took my way
Each trifle under truest bars to thrust,
That to my use it might unusèd stay
From hands of falsehood, in sure wards of trust.
But thou, to whom my jewels trifles are,
Most worthy comfort, now my greatest grief,
Thou best of dearest and mine only care
Art left the prey of every vulgar thief.
Thee have I not locked up in any chest
Save where thou art not, though I feel thou art—
Within the gentle closure of my breast,
From whence at pleasure thou mayst come and part;
    And even thence thou wilt be stol'n, I fear,
    For truth proves thievish for a prize so dear.

Against that time—if ever that time come—
When I shall see thee frown on my defects,
Whenas thy love hath cast his utmost sum,
Called to that audit by advised respects;
Against that time when thou shalt strangely pass
And scarcely greet me with that sun, thine eye,
When love converted from the thing it was
Shall reasons find of settled gravity:
Against that time do I ensconce me here
Within the knowledge of mine own desert,
And this my hand against myself uprear
To guard the lawful reasons on thy part.
    To leave poor me thou hast the strength of laws,
    Since why to love I can allege no cause.

How heavy do I journey on the way,
When what I seek—my weary travel's end—
Doth teach that ease and that repose to say
'Thus far the miles are measured from thy friend.'
The beast that bears me, tired with my woe,
Plods dully on to bear that weight in me,
As if by some instinct the wretch did know
His rider loved not speed, being made from thee.
The bloody spur cannot provoke him on
That sometimes anger thrusts into his hide,
Which heavily he answers with a groan
More sharp to me than spurring to his side;
 For that same groan doth put this in my mind:
 My grief lies onward and my joy behind.

Thus can my love excuse the slow offence
Of my dull bearer when from thee I speed:
From where thou art why should I haste me thence?
Till I return, of posting is no need.
O what excuse will my poor beast then find
When swift extremity can seem but slow?
Then should I spur, though mounted on the wind;
In wingèd speed no motion shall I know.
Then can no horse with my desire keep pace;
Therefore desire, of perfect'st love being made,
Shall rein no dull flesh in his fiery race;
But love, for love, thus shall excuse my jade:
 Since from thee going he went wilful-slow,
 Towards thee I'll run and give him leave to go.

So am I as the rich whose blessèd key
Can bring him to his sweet up-lockèd treasure,
The which he will not ev'ry hour survey,
For blunting the fine point of seldom pleasure.
Therefore are feasts so solemn and so rare
Since, seldom coming, in the long year set
Like stones of worth they thinly placèd are,
Or captain jewels in the carcanet.
So is the time that keeps you as my chest,
Or as the wardrobe which the robe doth hide,
To make some special instant special blest
By new unfolding his imprisoned pride.
    Blessèd are you whose worthiness gives scope,
    Being had, to triumph; being lacked, to hope.

What is your substance, whereof are you made,
That millions of strange shadows on you tend?
Since every one hath, every one, one shade,
And you, but one, can every shadow lend.
Describe Adonis, and the counterfeit
Is poorly imitated after you.
On Helen's cheek all art of beauty set,
And you in Grecian tires are painted new.
Speak of the spring and foison of the year:
The one doth shadow of your beauty show,
The other as your bounty doth appear;
And you in every blessèd shape we know.
  In all external grace you have some part,
  But you like none, none you, for constant heart.

O how much more doth beauty beauteous seem
By that sweet ornament which truth doth give!
The rose looks fair, but fairer we it deem
For that sweet odour which doth in it live.
The canker blooms have full as deep a dye
As the perfumèd tincture of the roses,
Hang on such thorns, and play as wantonly
When summer's breath their maskèd buds discloses;
But for their virtue only is their show
They live unwooed and unrespected fade,
Die to themselves. Sweet roses do not so;
Of their sweet deaths are sweetest odours made:
   And so of you, beauteous and lovely youth,
    When that shall fade, by verse distils your truth.

Not marble nor the gilded monuments
Of princes shall outlive this powerful rhyme,
But you shall shine more bright in these contents
Than unswept stone besmeared with sluttish time.
When wasteful war shall statues overturn,
And broils root out the work of masonry,
Nor Mars his sword nor war's quick fire shall burn
The living record of your memory.
'Gainst death and all oblivious enmity
Shall you pace forth; your praise shall still find room
Even in the eyes of all posterity
That wear this world out to the ending doom.
    So, till the judgement that yourself arise,
    You live in this, and dwell in lovers' eyes.

Sweet love, renew thy force. Be it not said
Thy edge should blunter be than appetite,
Which but today by feeding is allayed,
Tomorrow sharpened in his former might.
So, love, be thou; although today thou fill
Thy hungry eyes even till they wink with fullness,
Tomorrow see again, and do not kill
The spirit of love with a perpetual dullness.
Let this sad int'rim like the ocean be
Which parts the shore where two contracted new
Come daily to the banks, that when they see
Return of love, more blessed may be the view;
   Or call it winter, which, being full of care,
   Makes summer's welcome, thrice more wished,
      more rare.

Being your slave, what should I do but tend
Upon the hours and times of your desire?
I have no precious time at all to spend,
Nor services to do, till you require;
Nor dare I chide the world-without-end hour
Whilst I, my sovereign, watch the clock for you,
Nor think the bitterness of absence sour
When you have bid your servant once adieu.
Nor dare I question with my jealous thought
Where you may be, or your affairs suppose,
But like a sad slave stay and think of naught
Save, where you are, how happy you make those.
    So true a fool is love that in your will,
    Though you do anything, he thinks no ill.

That god forbid, that made me first your slave,
I should in thought control your times of pleasure,
Or at your hand th' account of hours to crave,
Being your vassal bound to stay your leisure.
O let me suffer, being at your beck,
Th'imprisoned absence of your liberty,
And patience, tame to sufferance, bide each check,
Without accusing you of injury.
Be where you list, your charter is so strong
That you yourself may privilege your time
To what you will; to you it doth belong
Yourself to pardon of self-doing crime.
   I am to wait, though waiting so be hell,
   Not blame your pleasure, be it ill or well.

If there be nothing new, but that which is
Hath been before, how are our brains beguiled,
Which, labouring for invention, bear amiss
The second burden of a former child!
O that record could with a backward look
Even of five hundred courses of the sun
Show me your image in some antique book
Since mind at first in character was done,
That I might see what the old world could say
To this composèd wonder of your frame;
Whether we are mended or whe'er better they,
Or whether revolution be the same.
    O, sure I am the wits of former days
    To subjects worse have given admiring praise.

Like as the waves make towards the pebbled shore,
So do our minutes hasten to their end,
Each changing place with that which goes before;
In sequent toil all forwards do contend.
Nativity, once in the main of light,
Crawls to maturity, wherewith being crowned
Crookèd eclipses 'gainst his glory fight,
And time that gave doth now his gift confound.
Time doth transfix the flourish set on youth,
And delves the parallels in beauty's brow;
Feeds on the rarities of nature's truth,
And nothing stands but for his scythe to mow.
   And yet to times in hope my verse shall stand,
    Praising thy worth despite his cruel hand.

Is it thy will thy image should keep open
My heavy eyelids to the weary night?
Dost thou desire my slumbers should be broken
While shadows like to thee do mock my sight?
Is it thy spirit that thou send'st from thee
So far from home into my deeds to pry,
To find out shames and idle hours in me,
The scope and tenor of thy jealousy?
O no; thy love, though much, is not so great.
It is my love that keeps mine eye awake,
Mine own true love that doth my rest defeat,
To play the watchman ever for thy sake.
    For thee watch I whilst thou dost wake elsewhere,
    From me far off, with others all too near.

Sin of self-love possesseth all mine eye,
And all my soul, and all my every part;
And for this sin there is no remedy,
It is so grounded inward in my heart.
Methinks no face so gracious is as mine,
No shape so true, no truth of such account,
And for myself mine own worth do define
As I all other in all worths surmount.
But when my glass shows me myself indeed,
Beated and chapped with tanned antiquity,
Mine own self-love quite contrary I read;
Self so self-loving were iniquity.
   'Tis thee, my self, that for myself I praise,
   Painting my age with beauty of thy days.

Against my love shall be as I am now,
With time's injurious hand crushed and o'erworn;
When hours have drained his blood and filled his brow
With lines and wrinkles; when his youthful morn
Hath travelled on to age's steepy night,
And all those beauties whereof now he's king
Are vanishing, or vanished out of sight,
Stealing away the treasure of his spring:
For such a time do I now fortify
Against confounding age's cruel knife,
That he shall never cut from memory
My sweet love's beauty, though my lover's life.
  His beauty shall in these black lines be seen,
  And they shall live, and he in them still green.

When I have seen by time's fell hand defaced
The rich proud cost of outworn buried age;
When sometime-lofty towers I see down razed,
And brass eternal slave to mortal rage;
When I have seen the hungry ocean gain
Advantage on the kingdom of the shore,
And the firm soil win of the wat'ry main,
Increasing store with loss and loss with store;
When I have seen such interchange of state,
Or state itself confounded to decay,
Ruin hath taught me thus to ruminate:
That time will come and take my love away.
    This thought is as a death, which cannot choose
    But weep to have that which it fears to lose.

Since brass, nor stone, nor earth, nor boundless sea,
But sad mortality o'ersways their power,
How with this rage shall beauty hold a plea,
Whose action is no stronger than a flower?
O how shall summer's honey breath hold out
Against the wrackful siege of battering days
When rocks impregnable are not so stout,
Nor gates of steel so strong, but time decays?
O fearful meditation! Where, alack,
Shall time's best jewel from time's chest lie hid,
Or what strong hand can hold his swift foot back,
Or who his spoil of beauty can forbid?
    O none, unless this miracle have might:
    That in black ink my love may still shine bright.

Tired with all these, for restful death I cry:
As, to behold desert a beggar born,
And needy nothing trimmed in jollity,
And purest faith unhappily forsworn,
And gilded honour shamefully misplaced,
And maiden virtue rudely strumpeted,
And right perfection wrongfully disgraced,
And strength by limping sway disablèd,
And art made tongue-tied by authority,
And folly, doctor-like, controlling skill,
And simple truth miscalled simplicity,
And captive good attending captain ill.
　　Tired with all these, from these would I be gone,
　　Save that to die I leave my love alone.

Ah, wherefore with infection should he live
And with his presence grace impiety,
That sin by him advantage should achieve
And lace itself with his society?
Why should false painting imitate his cheek,
And steal dead seeming of his living hue?
Why should poor beauty indirectly seek
Roses of shadow, since his rose is true?
Why should he live now nature bankrupt is,
Beggared of blood to blush through lively veins,
For she hath no exchequer now but his,
And proud of many, lives upon his gains?
    O, him she stores to show what wealth she had
    In days long since, before these last so bad.

Thus is his cheek the map of days outworn,
When beauty lived and died as flowers do now,
Before these bastard signs of fair were borne
Or durst inhabit on a living brow;
Before the golden tresses of the dead,
The right of sepulchres, were shorn away
To live a second life on second head;
Ere beauty's dead fleece made another gay.
In him those holy antique hours are seen
Without all ornament, itself and true,
Making no summer of another's green,
Robbing no old to dress his beauty new;
    And him as for a map doth nature store,
    To show false art what beauty was of yore.

Those parts of thee that the world's eye doth view
Want nothing that the thought of hearts can mend.
All tongues, the voice of souls, give thee that due,
Utt'ring bare truth even so as foes commend.
Thy outward thus with outward praise is crowned,
But those same tongues that give thee so thine own
In other accents do this praise confound
By seeing farther than the eye hath shown.
They look into the beauty of thy mind,
And that in guess they measure by thy deeds.
Then, churls, their thoughts—although their eyes
        were kind—
To thy fair flower add the rank smell of weeds.
    But why thy odour matcheth not thy show,
    The soil is this: that thou dost common grow.

That thou are blamed shall not be thy defect,
For slander's mark was ever yet the fair.
The ornament of beauty is suspect,
A crow that flies in heaven's sweetest air.
So thou be good, slander doth but approve
Thy worth the greater, being wooed of time;
For canker vice the sweetest buds doth love,
And thou present'st a pure unstainèd prime.
Thou hast passed by the ambush of young days
Either not assailed, or victor being charged;
Yet this thy praise cannot be so thy praise
To tie up envy, evermore enlarged.
   If some suspect of ill masked not thy show,
    Then thou alone kingdoms of hearts shouldst owe.

No longer mourn for me when I am dead
Than you shall hear the surly sullen bell
Give warning to the world that I am fled
From this vile world with vilest worms to dwell.
Nay, if you read this line, remember not
The hand that writ it; for I love you so
That I in your sweet thoughts would be forgot
If thinking on me then should make you woe.
O, if, I say, you look upon this verse
When I perhaps compounded am with clay,
Do not so much as my poor name rehearse,
But let your love even with my life decay,
    Lest the wise world should look into your moan
    And mock you with me after I am gone.

O, lest the world should task you to recite
What merit lived in me that you should love,
After my death, dear love, forget me quite;
For you in me can nothing worthy prove—
Unless you would devise some virtuous lie
To do more for me than mine own desert,
And hang more praise upon deceasèd I
Than niggard truth would willingly impart.
O, lest your true love may seem false in this,
That you for love speak well of me untrue,
My name be buried where my body is,
And live no more to shame nor me nor you;
   For I am shamed by that which I bring forth,
   And so should you, to love things nothing worth.

That time of year thou mayst in me behold
When yellow leaves, or none, or few, do hang
Upon those boughs which shake against the cold,
Bare ruined choirs where late the sweet birds sang.
In me thou seest the twilight of such day
As after sunset fadeth in the west,
Which by and by black night doth take away,
Death's second self, that seals up all in rest.
In me thou seest the glowing of such fire
That on the ashes of his youth doth lie
As the death-bed whereon it must expire,
Consumed with that which it was nourished by.
    This thou perceiv'st, which makes thy love more
        strong,
    To love that well which thou must leave ere long.

But be contented when that fell arrest
Without all bail shall carry me away.
My life hath in this line some interest,
Which for memorial still with thee shall stay.
When thou reviewest this, thou dost review
The very part was consecrate to thee.
The earth can have but earth, which is his due;
My spirit is thine, the better part of me.
So then thou hast but lost the dregs of life,
The prey of worms, my body being dead,
The coward conquest of a wretch's knife,
Too base of thee to be rememberèd.
    The worth of that is that which it contains,
    And that is this, and this with thee remains.

So are you to my thoughts as food to life,
Or as sweet-seasoned showers are to the ground;
And for the peace of you I hold such strife
As 'twixt a miser and his wealth is found:
Now proud as an enjoyer, and anon
Doubting the filching age will steal his treasure;
Now counting best to be with you alone,
Then bettered that the world may see my pleasure;
Sometime all full with feasting on your sight,
And by and by clean starvèd for a look;
Possessing or pursuing no delight
Save what is had or must from you be took.
   Thus do I pine and surfeit day by day,
   Or gluttoning on all, or all away.

Why is my verse so barren of new pride,
So far from variation or quick change?
Why, with the time, do I not glance aside
To new-found methods and to compounds strange?
Why write I still all one, ever the same,
And keep invention in a noted weed,
That every word doth almost tell my name,
Showing their birth and where they did proceed?
O know, sweet love, I always write of you,
And you and love are still my argument;
So all my best is dressing old words new,
Spending again what is already spent;
    For as the sun is daily new and old,
    So is my love, still telling what is told.

Thy glass will show thee how thy beauties wear,
Thy dial how thy precious minutes waste,
The vacant leaves thy mind's imprint will bear,
And of this book this learning mayst thou taste:
The wrinkles which thy glass will truly show
Of mouthèd graves will give thee memory;
Thou by thy dial's shady stealth mayst know
Time's thievish progress to eternity;
Look what thy memory cannot contain
Commit to these waste blanks, and thou shalt find
Those children nursed, delivered from thy brain,
To take a new acquaintance of thy mind.
   These offices so oft as thou wilt look
   Shall profit thee and much enrich thy book.

So oft have I invoked thee for my muse
And found such fair assistance in my verse
As every alien pen hath got my use,
And under thee their poesy disperse.
Thine eyes, that taught the dumb on high to sing
And heavy ignorance aloft to fly,
Have added feathers to the learned's wing
And given grace a double majesty.
Yet be most proud of that which I compile,
Whose influence is thine and born of thee.
In others' works thou dost but mend the style,
And arts with thy sweet graces gracèd be;
   But thou art all my art, and dost advance
   As high as learning my rude ignorance.

Whilst I alone did call upon thy aid
My verse alone had all thy gentle grace;
But now my gracious numbers are decayed,
And my sick muse doth give another place.
I grant, sweet love, thy lovely argument
Deserves the travail of a worthier pen,
Yet what of thee thy poet doth invent
He robs thee of, and pays it thee again.
He lends thee virtue, and he stole that word
From thy behaviour; beauty doth he give,
And found it in thy cheek: he can afford
No praise to thee but what in thee doth live.
    Then thank him not for that which he doth say,
    Since what he owes thee thou thyself dost pay.

O, how I faint when I of you do write,
Knowing a better spirit doth use your name,
And in the praise thereof spends all his might,
To make me tongue-tied, speaking of your fame!
But since your worth, wide as the ocean is,
The humble as the proudest sail doth bear,
My saucy barque, inferior far to his,
On your broad main doth wilfully appear.
Your shallowest help will hold me up afloat
Whilst he upon your soundless deep doth ride;
Or, being wrecked, I am a worthless boat,
He of tall building and of goodly pride.
    Then if he thrive and I be cast away,
    The worst was this: my love was my decay.

Or I shall live your epitaph to make,
Or you survive when I in earth am rotten.
From hence your memory death cannot take,
Although in me each part will be forgotten.
Your name from hence immortal life shall have,
Though I, once gone, to all the world must die.
The earth can yield me but a common grave
When you entombèd in men's eyes shall lie.
Your monument shall be my gentle verse,
Which eyes not yet created shall o'er-read,
And tongues to be your being shall rehearse
When all the breathers of this world are dead.
    You still shall live—such virtue hath my pen—
    Where breath most breathes, even in the mouths
        of men.

I grant thou wert not married to my muse,
And therefore mayst without attaint o'erlook
The dedicated words which writers use
Of their fair subject, blessing every book.
Thou art as fair in knowledge as in hue,
Finding thy worth a limit past my praise,
And therefore art enforced to seek anew
Some fresher stamp of these time-bettering days.
And do so, love; yet when they have devised
What strainèd touches rhetoric can lend,
Thou, truly fair, wert truly sympathized
In true plain words by thy true-telling friend;
    And their gross painting might be better used
    Where cheeks need blood: in thee it is abused.

I never saw that you did painting need,
And therefore to your fair no painting set.
I found—or thought I found—you did exceed
The barren tender of a poet's debt;
And therefore have I slept in your report:
That you yourself, being extant, well might show
How far a modern quill doth come too short,
Speaking of worth, what worth in you doth grow.
This silence for my sin you did impute,
Which shall be most my glory, being dumb;
For I impair not beauty, being mute,
When others would give life, and bring a tomb.
    There lives more life in one of your fair eyes
    Than both your poets can in praise devise.

Who is it that says most which can say more
Than this rich praise: that you alone are you,
In whose confine immurèd is the store
Which should example where your equal grew?
Lean penury within that pen doth dwell
That to his subject lends not some small glory;
But he that writes of you, if he can tell
That you are you, so dignifies his story.
Let him but copy what in you is writ,
Not making worse what nature made so clear,
And such a counterpart shall fame his wit,
Making his style admirèd everywhere.
    You to your beauteous blessings add a curse,
    Being fond on praise, which makes your praises
        worse.

My tongue-tied muse in manners holds her still
While comments of your praise, richly compiled,
Reserve thy character with golden quill
And precious phrase by all the muses filed.
I think good thoughts whilst other write good words,
And like unlettered clerk still cry 'Amen'
To every hymn that able spirit affords
In polished form of well-refinèd pen.
Hearing you praised I say ''Tis so, 'tis true,'
And to the most of praise add something more;
But that is in my thought, whose love to you,
Though words come hindmost, holds his rank before.
   Then others for the breath of words respect,
   Me for my dumb thoughts, speaking in effect.

Was it the proud full sail of his great verse
Bound for the prize of all-too-precious you
That did my ripe thoughts in my brain inhearse,
Making their tomb the womb wherein they grew?
Was it his spirit, by spirits taught to write
Above a mortal pitch, that struck me dead?
No, neither he nor his compeers by night
Giving him aid, my verse astonishèd.
He nor that affable familiar ghost
Which nightly gulls him with intelligence,
As victors, of my silence cannot boast;
I was not sick of any fear from thence.
    But when your countenance filled up his line,
    Then lacked I matter; that enfeebled mine.

Farewell—thou art too dear for my possessing,
And like enough thou know'st thy estimate.
The charter of thy worth gives thee releasing;
My bonds in thee are all determinate.
For how do I hold thee but by thy granting,
And for that riches where is my deserving?
The cause of this fair gift in me is wanting,
And so my patent back again is swerving.
Thyself thou gav'st, thy own worth then not knowing,
Or me to whom thou gav'st it else mistaking;
So thy great gift, upon misprision growing,
Comes home again, on better judgement making.
    Thus have I had thee as a dream doth flatter:
    In sleep a king, but waking no such matter.

When thou shalt be disposed to set me light
And place my merit in the eye of scorn,
Upon thy side against myself I'll fight,
And prove thee virtuous though thou art forsworn.
With mine own weakness being best acquainted,
Upon thy part I can set down a story
Of faults concealed wherein I am attainted,
That thou in losing me shall win much glory;
And I by this will be a gainer too;
For bending all my loving thoughts on thee,
The injuries that to myself I do,
Doing thee vantage, double vantage me.
     Such is my love, to thee I so belong,
     That for thy right myself will bear all wrong.

Say that thou didst forsake me for some fault,
And I will comment upon that offence;
Speak of my lameness, and I straight will halt,
Against thy reasons making no defence.
Thou canst not, love, disgrace me half so ill,
To set a form upon desirèd change,
As I'll myself disgrace, knowing thy will.
I will acquaintance strangle and look strange,
Be absent from thy walks, and in my tongue
Thy sweet belovèd name no more shall dwell,
Lest I, too much profane, should do it wrong,
And haply of our old acquaintance tell.
   For thee, against myself I'll vow debate;
   For I must ne'er love him whom thou dost hate.

Then hate me when thou wilt, if ever, now,
Now while the world is bent my deeds to cross,
Join with the spite of fortune, make me bow,
And do not drop in for an after-loss.
Ah do not, when my heart hath scaped this sorrow,
Come in the rearward of a conquered woe;
Give not a windy night a rainy morrow
To linger out a purposed overthrow.
If thou wilt leave me, do not leave me last,
When other petty griefs have done their spite,
But in the onset come; so shall I taste
At first the very worst of fortune's might,
   And other strains of woe, which now seem woe,
   Compared with loss of thee will not seem so.

Some glory in their birth, some in their skill,
Some in their wealth, some in their body's force,
Some in their garments (though new-fangled ill),
Some in their hawks and hounds, some in their horse,
And every humour hath his adjunct pleasure
Wherein it finds a joy above the rest.
But these particulars are not my measure;
All these I better in one general best.
Thy love is better than high birth to me,
Richer than wealth, prouder than garments' cost,
Of more delight than hawks or horses be,
And having thee of all men's pride I boast,
    Wretched in this alone: that thou mayst take
    All this away, and me most wretched make.

But do thy worst to steal thyself away,
For term of life thou art assurèd mine,
And life no longer than thy love will stay,
For it depends upon that love of thine.
Then need I not to fear the worst of wrongs
When in the least of them my life hath end.
I see a better state to me belongs
Than that which on thy humour doth depend.
Thou canst not vex me with inconstant mind,
Since that my life on thy revolt doth lie.
O, what a happy title do I find—
Happy to have thy love, happy to die!
　　But what's so blessèd fair that fears no blot?
　　Thou mayst be false, and yet I know it not.

So shall I live supposing thou art true
Like a deceivèd husband; so love's face
May still seem love to me, though altered new—
Thy looks with me, thy heart in other place.
For there can live no hatred in thine eye,
Therefore in that I cannot know thy change.
In many's looks the false heart's history
Is writ in moods and frowns and wrinkles strange;
But heaven in thy creation did decree
That in thy face sweet love should ever dwell;
Whate'er thy thoughts or thy heart's workings be,
Thy looks should nothing thence but sweetness tell.
   How like Eve's apple doth thy beauty grow
   If thy sweet virtue answer not thy show!

They that have power to hurt and will do none,
That do not do the thing they most do show,
Who moving others are themselves as stone,
Unmovèd, cold, and to temptation slow—
They rightly do inherit heaven's graces,
And husband nature's riches from expense;
They are the lords and owners of their faces,
Others but stewards of their excellence.
The summer's flower is to the summer sweet
Though to itself it only live and die,
But if that flower with base infection meet
The basest weed outbraves his dignity;
    For sweetest things turn sourest by their deeds:
    Lilies that fester smell far worse than weeds.

How sweet and lovely dost thou make the shame
Which, like a canker in the fragrant rose,
Doth spot the beauty of thy budding name!
O, in what sweets dost thou thy sins enclose!
That tongue that tells the story of thy days,
Making lascivious comments on thy sport,
Cannot dispraise, but in a kind of praise,
Naming thy name, blesses an ill report.
O, what a mansion have those vices got
Which for their habitation chose out thee,
Where beauty's veil doth cover every blot
And all things turns to fair that eyes can see!
   Take heed, dear heart, of this large privilege:
   The hardest knife ill used doth lose his edge.

Some say thy fault is youth, some wantonness;
Some say thy grace is youth and gentle sport.
Both grace and faults are loved of more and less;
Thou mak'st faults graces that to thee resort.
As on the finger of a thronèd queen
The basest jewel will be well esteemed,
So are those errors that in thee are seen
To truths translated and for true things deemed.
How many lambs might the stern wolf betray
If like a lamb he could his looks translate!
How many gazers mightst thou lead away
If thou wouldst use the strength of all thy state!
    But do not so: I love thee in such sort
    As, thou being mine, mine is thy good report.

How like a winter hath my absence been
From thee, the pleasure of the fleeting year!
What freezings have I felt, what dark days seen,
What old December's bareness everywhere!
And yet this time removed was summer's time,
The teeming autumn big with rich increase,
Bearing the wanton burden of the prime
Like widowed wombs after their lords' decease.
Yet this abundant issue seemed to me
But hope of orphans and unfathered fruit,
For summer and his pleasures wait on thee,
And thou away, the very birds are mute;
    Or if they sing, 'tis with so dull a cheer
    That leaves look pale, dreading the winter's near.

From you have I been absent in the spring
When proud-pied April, dressed in all his trim,
Hath put a spirit of youth in everything,
That heavy Saturn laughed and leapt with him.
Yet nor the lays of birds nor the sweet smell
Of different flowers in odour and in hue
Could make me any summer's story tell,
Or from their proud lap pluck them where they grew;
Nor did I wonder at the lily's white,
Nor praise the deep vermilion in the rose.
They were but sweet, but figures of delight
Drawn after you, you pattern of all those;
    Yet seemed it winter still, and, you away,
    As with your shadow I with these did play.

The forward violet thus did I chide:
Sweet thief, whence didst thou steal thy sweet
    that smells,
If not from my love's breath? The purple pride
Which on thy soft cheek for complexion dwells
In my love's veins thou hast too grossly dyed.
The lily I condemnèd for thy hand,
And buds of marjoram had stol'n thy hair;
The roses fearfully on thorns did stand,
One blushing shame, another white despair;
A third, nor red nor white, had stol'n of both,
And to his robb'ry had annexed thy breath;
But for his theft in pride of all his growth
A vengeful canker ate him up to death.
    More flowers I noted, yet I none could see
    But sweet or colour it had stol'n from thee.

Where art thou, muse, that thou forget'st so long
To speak of that which gives thee all thy might?
Spend'st thou thy fury on some worthless song,
Dark'ning thy power to lend base subjects light?
Return, forgetful muse, and straight redeem
In gentle numbers time so idly spent;
Sing to the ear that doth thy lays esteem
And gives thy pen both skill and argument.
Rise, resty muse, my love's sweet face survey
If time have any wrinkle graven there.
If any, be a satire to decay
And make time's spoils despisèd everywhere.
    Give my love fame faster than time wastes life;
      So, thou prevene'st his scythe and crookèd knife.

O truant muse, what shall be thy amends
For thy neglect of truth in beauty dyed?
Both truth and beauty on my love depends;
So dost thou too, and therein dignified.
Make answer, muse. Wilt thou not haply say
'Truth needs no colour with his colour fixed,
Beauty no pencil beauty's truth to lay,
But best is best if never intermixed'?
Because he needs no praise wilt thou be dumb?
Excuse not silence so, for't lies in thee
To make him much outlive a gilded tomb,
And to be praised of ages yet to be.
   Then do thy office, muse; I teach thee how
   To make him seem long hence as he shows now.

My love is strengthened, though more weak in
    seeming.
I love not less, though less the show appear.
That love is merchandized whose rich esteeming
The owner's tongue doth publish everywhere.
Our love was new and then but in the spring
When I was wont to greet it with my lays,
As Philomel in summer's front doth sing,
And stops her pipe in growth of riper days—
Not that the summer is less pleasant now
Than when her mournful hymns did hush the night,
But that wild music burdens every bough,
And sweets grown common lose their dear delight.
    Therefore like her I sometime hold my tongue,
    Because I would not dull you with my song.

Alack, what poverty my muse brings forth
That, having such a scope to show her pride,
The argument all bare is of more worth
Than when it hath my added praise beside!
O blame me not if I no more can write!
Look in your glass and there appears a face
That overgoes my blunt invention quite,
Dulling my lines and doing me disgrace.
Were it not sinful then, striving to mend,
To mar the subject that before was well?—
For to no other pass my verses tend
Than of your graces and your gifts to tell;
    And more, much more, than in my verse can sit
    Your own glass shows you when you look in it.

To me, fair friend, you never can be old;
For as you were when first your eye I eyed,
Such seems your beauty still. Three winters cold
Have from the forests shook three summers' pride;
Three beauteous springs to yellow autumn turned
In process of the seasons have I seen,
Three April perfumes in three hot Junes burned
Since first I saw you fresh, which yet are green.
Ah yet doth beauty, like a dial hand,
Steal from his figure and no pace perceived;
So your sweet hue, which methinks still doth stand,
Hath motion, and mine eye may be deceived.
    For fear of which, hear this, thou age unbred:
    Ere you were born was beauty's summer dead.

Let not my love be called idolatry,
Nor my belovèd as an idol show,
Since all alike my songs and praises be
To one, of one, still such, and ever so.
Kind is my love today, tomorrow kind,
Still constant in a wondrous excellence.
Therefore my verse, to constancy confined,
One thing expressing, leaves out difference.
'Fair, kind, and true' is all my argument,
'Fair, kind, and true' varying to other words,
And in this change is my invention spent,
Three themes in one, which wondrous scope affords.
    Fair, kind, and true have often lived alone,
    Which three till now never kept seat in one.

When in the chronicle of wasted time
I see descriptions of the fairest wights,
And beauty making beautiful old rhyme
In praise of ladies dead and lovely knights;
Then in the blazon of sweet beauty's best,
Of hand, of foot, of lip, of eye, of brow,
I see their antique pen would have expressed
Ev'n such a beauty as you master now.
So all their praises are but prophecies
Of this our time, all you prefiguring,
And for they looked but with divining eyes
They had not skill enough your worth to sing;
   For we which now behold these present days
   Have eyes to wonder, but lack tongues to praise.

Not mine own fears nor the prophetic soul
Of the wide world dreaming on things to come
Can yet the lease of my true love control,
Supposed as forfeit to a confined doom.
The mortal moon hath her eclipse endured,
And the sad augurs mock their own presage;
Incertainties now crown themselves assured,
And peace proclaims olives of endless age.
Now with the drops of this most balmy time
My love looks fresh, and death to me subscribes,
Since spite of him I'll live in this poor rhyme
While he insults o'er dull and speechless tribes;
    And thou in this shalt find thy monument
     When tyrants' crests and tombs of brass are spent.

What's in the brain that ink may character
Which hath not figured to thee my true spirit?
What's new to speak, what now to register,
That may express my love or thy dear merit?
Nothing, sweet boy; but yet like prayers divine
I must each day say o'er the very same,
Counting no old thing old, thou mine, I thine,
Even as when first I hallowed thy fair name.
So that eternal love in love's fresh case
Weighs not the dust and injury of age,
Nor gives to necessary wrinkles place,
But makes antiquity for aye his page,
    Finding the first conceit of love there bred
    Where time and outward form would show it dead.

O never say that I was false of heart,
Though absence seemed my flame to qualify—
As easy might I from myself depart
As from my soul, which in thy breast doth lie.
That is my home of love. If I have ranged,
Like him that travels I return again,
Just to the time, not with the time exchanged,
So that myself bring water for my stain.
Never believe, though in my nature reigned
All frailties that besiege all kinds of blood,
That it could so preposterously be stained
To leave for nothing all thy sum of good;
  For nothing this wide universe I call
  Save thou my rose; in it thou art my all.

Alas, 'tis true, I have gone here and there
And made myself a motley to the view,
Gored mine own thoughts, sold cheap what is most
    dear,
Made old offences of affections new.
Most true it is that I have looked on truth
Askance and strangely. But, by all above,
These blenches gave my heart another youth,
And worse essays proved thee my best of love.
Now all is done, have what shall have no end;
Mine appetite I never more will grind
On newer proof to try an older friend,
A god in love, to whom I am confined.
    Then give me welcome, next my heaven the best,
    Even to thy pure and most most loving breast.

O, for my sake do you with fortune chide,
The guilty goddess of my harmful deeds,
That did not better for my life provide
Than public means which public manners breeds.
Thence comes it that my name receives a brand,
And almost thence my nature is subdued
To what it works in, like the dyer's hand.
Pity me then, and wish I were renewed,
Whilst like a willing patient I will drink
Potions of eisel 'gainst my strong infection;
No bitterness that I will bitter think,
Nor double penance to correct correction.
    Pity me then, dear friend, and I assure ye
    Even that your pity is enough to cure me.

Your love and pity doth th'impression fill
Which vulgar scandal stamped upon my brow;
For what care I who calls me well or ill,
So you o'er-green my bad, my good allow?
You are my all the world, and I must strive
To know my shames and praises from your tongue—
None else to me, nor I to none alive,
That my steeled sense or changes, right or wrong.
In so profound abyss I throw all care
Of others' voices that my adder's sense
To critic and to flatterer stoppèd are.
Mark how with my neglect I do dispense:
    You are so strongly in my purpose bred
    That all the world besides, methinks, they're dead.

Since I left you mine eye is in my mind,
And that which governs me to go about
Doth part his function and is partly blind,
Seems seeing, but effectually is out;
For it no form delivers to the heart
Of bird, of flower, or shape which it doth latch.
Of his quick objects hath the mind no part,
Nor his own vision holds what it doth catch;
For if it see the rud'st or gentlest sight,
The most sweet favour or deformèd'st creature,
The mountain or the sea, the day or night,
The crow or dove, it shapes them to your feature.
　　Incapable of more, replete with you,
　　My most true mind thus makes mine eye untrue.

Or whether doth my mind, being crowned with you,
Drink up the monarch's plague, this flattery,
Or whether shall I say mine eye saith true,
And that your love taught it this alchemy,
To make of monsters and things indigest
Such cherubins as your sweet self resemble,
Creating every bad a perfect best
As fast as objects to his beams assemble?
O, 'tis the first, 'tis flatt'ry in my seeing,
And my great mind most kingly drinks it up.
Mine eye well knows what with his gust is 'greeing,
And to his palate doth prepare the cup.
   If it be poisoned, 'tis the lesser sin
   That mine eye loves it and doth first begin.

Those lines that I before have writ do lie,
Even those that said I could not love you dearer;
Yet then my judgement knew no reason why
My most full flame should afterwards burn clearer.
But reckoning time, whose millioned accidents
Creep in 'twixt vows and change decrees of kings,
Tan sacred beauty, blunt the sharp'st intents,
Divert strong minds to th' course of alt'ring things—
Alas, why, fearing of time's tyranny,
Might I not then say 'Now I love you best',
When I was certain o'er incertainty,
Crowning the present, doubting of the rest?
    Love is a babe; then might I not say so,
    To give full growth to that which still doth grow.

Let me not to the marriage of true minds
Admit impediments. Love is not love
Which alters when it alteration finds,
Or bends with the remover to remove.
O no, it is an ever fixèd mark
That looks on tempests and is never shaken;
It is the star to every wand'ring barque,
Whose worth's unknown although his height be
     taken.
Love's not time's fool, though rosy lips and cheeks
Within his bending sickle's compass come;
Love alters not with his brief hours and weeks,
But bears it out even to the edge of doom.
   If this be error and upon me proved,
   I never writ, nor no man ever loved.

Accuse me thus: that I have scanted all
Wherein I should your great deserts repay,
Forgot upon your dearest love to call
Whereto all bonds do tie me day by day;
That I have frequent been with unknown minds,
And given to time your own dear-purchased right;
That I have hoisted sail to all the winds
Which should transport me farthest from your sight.
Book both my wilfulness and errors down,
And on just proof surmise accumulate;
Bring me within the level of your frown,
But shoot not at me in your wakened hate,
    Since my appeal says I did strive to prove
    The constancy and virtue of your love.

Like as, to make our appetites more keen,
With eager compounds we our palate urge;
As to prevent our maladies unseen
We sicken to shun sickness when we purge:
Even so, being full of your ne'er cloying sweetness,
To bitter sauces did I frame my feeding,
And, sick of welfare, found a kind of meetness
To be diseased ere that there was true needing.
Thus policy in love, t'anticipate
The ills that were not, grew to faults assured,
And brought to medicine a healthful state
Which, rank of goodness, would by ill be cured.
　　But thence I learn, and find the lesson true:
　　Drugs poison him that so fell sick of you.

What potions have I drunk of siren tears
Distilled from limbecks foul as hell within,
Applying fears to hopes and hopes to fears,
Still losing when I saw myself to win!
What wretched errors hath my heart committed
Whilst it hath thought itself so blessèd never!
How have mine eyes out of their spheres been fitted
In the distraction of this madding fever!
O benefit of ill! Now I find true
That better is by evil still made better,
And ruined love when it is built anew
Grows fairer than at first, more strong, far greater.
　　So I return rebuked to my content,
　　And gain by ills thrice more than I have spent.

That you were once unkind befriends me now,
And for that sorrow which I then did feel
Needs must I under my transgression bow,
Unless my nerves were brass or hammered steel.
For if you were by my unkindness shaken
As I by yours, you've past a hell of time,
And I, a tyrant, have no leisure taken
To weigh how once I suffered in your crime.
O that our night of woe might have remembered
My deepest sense how hard true sorrow hits,
And soon to you as you to me then tendered
The humble salve which wounded bosoms fits!
    But that your trespass now becomes a fee;
    Mine ransoms yours, and yours must ransom me.

'Tis better to be vile than vile esteemed
When not to be receives reproach of being,
And the just pleasure lost, which is so deemed
Not by our feeling but by others' seeing.
For why should others' false adulterate eyes
Give salutation to my sportive blood?
Or on my frailties why are frailer spies,
Which in their wills count bad what I think good?
No, I am that I am, and they that level
At my abuses reckon up their own.
I may be straight, though they themselves be bevel;
By their rank thoughts my deeds must not be shown,
    Unless this general evil they maintain:
    All men are bad and in their badness reign.

Thy gift, thy tables, are within my brain
Full charactered with lasting memory,
Which shall above that idle rank remain
Beyond all date, even to eternity;
Or at the least so long as brain and heart
Have faculty by nature to subsist,
Till each to razed oblivion yield his part
Of thee, thy record never can be missed.
That poor retention could not so much hold,
Nor need I tallies thy dear love to score;
Therefore to give them from me was I bold,
To trust those tables that receive thee more.
    To keep an adjunct to remember thee
    Were to import forgetfulness in me.

No, time, thou shalt not boast that I do change!
Thy pyramids built up with newer might
To me are nothing novel, nothing strange,
They are but dressings of a former sight.
Our dates are brief, and therefore we admire
What thou dost foist upon us that is old,
And rather make them born to our desire
Than think that we before have heard them told.
Thy registers and thee I both defy,
Not wond'ring at the present nor the past;
For thy records and what we see doth lie,
Made more or less by thy continual haste.
   This I do vow, and this shall ever be:
   I will be true despite thy scythe and thee.

If my dear love were but the child of state
It might for fortune's bastard be unfathered,
As subject to time's love or to time's hate,
Weeds among weeds or flowers with flowers gathered.
No, it was builded far from accident;
It suffers not in smiling pomp, nor falls
Under the blow of thrallèd discontent
Whereto th'inviting time our fashion calls.
It fears not policy, that heretic
Which works on leases of short-numbered hours,
But all alone stands hugely politic,
That it nor grows with heat nor drowns with showers.
   To this I witness call the fools of time,
   Which die for goodness, who have lived for crime.

Were't aught to me I bore the canopy,
With my extern the outward honouring,
Or laid great bases for eternity
Which proves more short than waste or ruining?
Have I not seen dwellers on form and favour
Lose all and more by paying too much rent,
For compound sweet forgoing simple savour,
Pitiful thrivers in their gazing spent?
No, let me be obsequious in thy heart,
And take thou my oblation, poor but free,
Which is not mixed with seconds, knows no art
But mutual render, only me for thee.
    Hence, thou suborned informer! A true soul
    When most impeached stands least in thy control.

O thou my lovely boy, who in thy power
Dost hold time's fickle glass, his sickle-hour;
Who hast by waning grown, and therein show'st
Thy lovers withering as thy sweet self grow'st—
If nature, sovereign mistress over wrack,
As thou goest onwards still will pluck thee back,
She keeps thee to this purpose: that her skill
May time disgrace, and wretched minutes kill.
Yet fear her, O thou minion of her pleasure!
She may detain but not still keep her treasure.
    Her audit, though delayed, answered must be,
    And her quietus is to render thee.

In the old age black was not counted fair,
Or if it were, it bore not beauty's name;
But now is black beauty's successive heir,
And beauty slandered with a bastard shame:
For since each hand hath put on nature's power,
Fairing the foul with art's false borrowed face,
Sweet beauty hath no name, no holy bower,
But is profaned, if not lives in disgrace.
Therefore my mistress' eyes are raven-black,
Her brow so suited, and they mourners seem
At such who, not born fair, no beauty lack,
Sland'ring creation with a false esteem.
   Yet so they mourn, becoming of their woe,
    That every tongue says beauty should look so.

How oft, when thou, my music, music play'st
Upon that blessèd wood whose motion sounds
With thy sweet fingers when thou gently sway'st
The wiry concord that mine ear confounds,
Do I envy those jacks that nimble leap
To kiss the tender inward of thy hand
Whilst my poor lips, which should that harvest reap,
At the wood's boldness by thee blushing stand!
To be so tickled they would change their state
And situation with those dancing chips
O'er whom thy fingers walk with gentle gait,
Making dead wood more blessed than living lips.
   Since saucy jacks so happy are in this,
   Give them thy fingers, me thy lips to kiss.

Th'expense of spirit in a waste of shame
Is lust in action; and till action, lust
Is perjured, murd'rous, bloody, full of blame,
Savage, extreme, rude, cruel, not to trust,
Enjoyed no sooner but despisèd straight,
Past reason hunted, and no sooner had
Past reason hated as a swallowed bait
On purpose laid to make the taker mad;
Mad in pursuit and in possession so,
Had, having, and in quest to have, extreme;
A bliss in proof and proved, a very woe;
Before, a joy proposed; behind, a dream.
 All this the world well knows, yet none knows well
 To shun the heaven that leads men to this hell.

My mistress' eyes are nothing like the sun;
Coral is far more red than her lips' red.
If snow be white, why then her breasts are dun;
If hairs be wires, black wires grow on her head.
I have seen roses damasked, red and white,
But no such roses see I in her cheeks;
And in some perfumes is there more delight
Than in the breath that from my mistress reeks.
I love to hear her speak, yet well I know
That music hath a far more pleasing sound.
I grant I never saw a goddess go:
My mistress when she walks treads on the ground.
   And yet, by heaven, I think my love as rare
   As any she belied with false compare.

Thou art as tyrannous so as thou art
As those whose beauties proudly make them cruel,
For well thou know'st to my dear doting heart
Thou art the fairest and most precious jewel.
Yet, in good faith, some say that thee behold
Thy face hath not the power to make love groan.
To say they err I dare not be so bold,
Although I swear it to myself alone;
And, to be sure that is not false I swear,
A thousand groans but thinking on thy face
One on another's neck do witness bear
Thy black is fairest in my judgement's place.
   In nothing art thou black save in thy deeds,
     And thence this slander, as I think, proceeds.

Thine eyes I love, and they, as pitying me—
Knowing thy heart torment me with disdain—
Have put on black, and loving mourners be,
Looking with pretty ruth upon my pain;
And truly, not the morning sun of heaven
Better becomes the gray cheeks of the east,
Nor that full star that ushers in the even
Doth half that glory to the sober west,
As those two mourning eyes become thy face.
O, let it then as well beseem thy heart
To mourn for me, since mourning doth thee grace,
And suit thy pity like in every part.
    Then will I swear beauty herself is black,
    And all they foul that thy complexion lack.

Beshrew that heart that makes my heart to groan
For that deep wound it gives my friend and me!
Is't not enough to torture me alone,
But slave to slavery my sweet'st friend must be?
Me from myself thy cruel eye hath taken,
And my next self thou harder hast engrossed.
Of him, myself, and thee I am forsaken—
A torment thrice threefold thus to be crossed.
Prison my heart in thy steel bosom's ward,
But then my friend's heart let my poor heart bail;
Whoe'er keeps me, let my heart be his guard;
Thou canst not then use rigour in my jail.
   And yet thou wilt; for I, being pent in thee,
   Perforce am thine, and all that is in me.

So, now I have confessed that he is thine,
And I myself am mortgaged to thy will,
Myself I'll forfeit, so that other mine
Thou wilt restore to be my comfort still.
But thou wilt not, nor he will not be free,
For thou art covetous, and he is kind.
He learned but surety-like to write for me
Under that bond that him as fast doth bind.
The statute of thy beauty thou wilt take,
Thou usurer that putt'st forth all to use,
And sue a friend came debtor for my sake;
So him I lose through my unkind abuse.
   Him have I lost; thou hast both him and me;
   He pays the whole, and yet am I not free.

Whoever hath her wish, thou hast thy Will,
And Will to boot, and Will in overplus.
More than enough am I that vex thee still,
To thy sweet will making addition thus.
Wilt thou, whose will is large and spacious,
Not once vouchsafe to hide my will in thine?
Shall will in others seem right gracious,
And in my will no fair acceptance shine?
The sea, all water, yet receives rain still,
And in abundance addeth to his store;
So thou, being rich in Will, add to thy Will
One will of mine to make thy large Will more.
　　Let no unkind no fair beseechers kill;
　　Think all but one, and me in that one Will.

If thy soul check thee that I come so near,
Swear to thy blind soul that I was thy Will,
And will, thy soul knows, is admitted there;
Thus far for love my love-suit, sweet, fulfil.
Will will fulfil the treasure of thy love,
Ay, fill it full with wills, and my will one.
In things of great receipt with ease we prove
Among a number one is reckoned none.
Then in the number let me pass untold,
Though in thy store's account I one must be;
For nothing hold me, so it please thee hold
That nothing me a something, sweet, to thee.
    Make but my name thy love, and love that still,
    And then thou lov'st me for my name is Will.

Thou blind fool love, what dost thou to mine eyes
That they behold and see not what they see?
They know what beauty is, see where it lies,
Yet what the best is take the worst to be.
If eyes corrupt by over-partial looks
Be anchored in the bay where all men ride,
Why of eyes' falsehood hast thou forgèd hooks
Whereto the judgement of my heart is tied?
Why should my heart think that a several plot
Which my heart knows the wide world's common
      place?—
Or mine eyes, seeing this, say this is not,
To put fair truth upon so foul a face?
    In things right true my heart and eyes have erred,
    And to this false plague are they now transferred.

When my love swears that she is made of truth
I do believe her though I know she lies,
That she might think me some untutored youth
Unlearnèd in the world's false subtleties.
Thus vainly thinking that she thinks me young,
Although she knows my days are past the best,
Simply I credit her false-speaking tongue;
On both sides thus is simple truth suppressed.
But wherefore says she not she is unjust,
And wherefore say not I that I am old?
O, love's best habit is in seeming trust,
And age in love loves not to have years told.
   Therefore I lie with her, and she with me,
   And in our faults by lies we flattered be.

O, call not me to justify the wrong
That thy unkindness lays upon my heart.
Wound me not with thine eye but with thy tongue;
Use power with power, and slay me not by art.
Tell me thou lov'st elsewhere, but in my sight,
Dear heart, forbear to glance thine eye aside.
What need'st thou wound with cunning when thy
     might
Is more than my o'erpressed defence can bide?
Let me excuse thee: 'Ah, my love well knows
Her pretty looks have been mine enemies,
And therefore from my face she turns my foes
That they elsewhere might dart their injuries.'
  Yet do not so; but since I am near slain,
  Kill me outright with looks, and rid my pain.

Be wise as thou art cruel; do not press
My tongue-tied patience with too much disdain,
Lest sorrow lend me words, and words express
The manner of my pity-wanting pain.
If I might teach thee wit, better it were,
Though not to love, yet, love, to tell me so—
As testy sick men when their deaths be near
No news but health from their physicians know.
For if I should despair I should grow mad,
And in my madness might speak ill of thee.
Now this ill-wresting world is grown so bad
Mad slanderers by mad ears believèd be.
    That I may not be so, nor thou belied,
      Bear thine eyes straight, though thy proud heart go
        wide.

In faith, I do not love thee with mine eyes,
For they in thee a thousand errors note;
But 'tis my heart that loves what they despise,
Who in despite of view is pleased to dote.
Nor are mine ears with thy tongue's tune delighted,
Nor tender feeling to base touches prone;
Nor taste nor smell desire to be invited
To any sensual feast with thee alone;
But my five wits nor my five senses can
Dissuade one foolish heart from serving thee,
Who leaves unswayed the likeness of a man,
Thy proud heart's slave and vassal-wretch to be.
   Only my plague thus far I count my gain:
   That she that makes me sin awards me pain.

Love is my sin, and thy dear virtue hate,
Hate of my sin grounded on sinful loving.
O, but with mine compare thou thine own state,
And thou shalt find it merits not reproving;
Or if it do, not from those lips of thine
That have profaned their scarlet ornaments
And sealed false bonds of love as oft as mine,
Robbed others' beds' revenues of their rents.
Be it lawful I love thee as thou lov'st those
Whom thine eyes woo as mine importune thee.
Root pity in thy heart, that when it grows
Thy pity may deserve to pitied be.
    If thou dost seek to have what thou dost hide,
    By self example mayst thou be denied!

Lo, as a care-full housewife runs to catch
One of her feathered creatures broke away,
Sets down her babe and makes all swift dispatch
In pursuit of the thing she would have stay,
Whilst her neglected child holds her in chase,
Cries to catch her whose busy care is bent
To follow that which flies before her face,
Not prizing her poor infant's discontent:
So runn'st thou after that which flies from thee,
Whilst I, thy babe, chase thee afar behind;
But if thou catch thy hope, turn back to me
And play the mother's part: kiss me, be kind.
   So will I pray that thou mayst have thy Will
   If thou turn back and my loud crying still.

Two loves I have, of comfort and despair,
Which like two spirits do suggest me still.
The better angel is a man right fair,
The worser spirit a woman coloured ill.
To win me soon to hell my female evil
Tempteth my better angel from my side,
And would corrupt my saint to be a devil,
Wooing his purity with her foul pride;
And whether that my angel be turned fiend
Suspect I may, yet not directly tell;
But being both from me, both to each friend,
I guess one angel in another's hell.
    Yet this shall I ne'er know, but live in doubt
    Till my bad angel fire my good one out.

Those lips that love's own hand did make
Breathed forth the sound that said 'I hate'
To me that languished for her sake;
But when she saw my woeful state,
Straight in her heart did mercy come,
Chiding that tongue that ever sweet
Was used in giving gentle doom,
And taught it thus anew to greet:
'I hate' she altered with an end
That followed it as gentle day
Doth follow night who, like a fiend,
From heaven to hell is flown away.
   'I hate' from hate away she threw,
   And saved my life, saying 'not you.'

Poor soul, the centre of my sinful earth,
[   ] these rebel powers that thee array;
Why dost thou pine within and suffer dearth,
Painting thy outward walls so costly gay?
Why so large cost, having so short a lease,
Dost thou upon thy fading mansion spend?
Shall worms, inheritors of this excess,
Eat up thy charge? Is this thy body's end?
Then, soul, live thou upon thy servant's loss,
And let that pine to aggravate thy store.
Buy terms divine in selling hours of dross;
Within be fed, without be rich no more.
　　So shalt thou feed on death, that feeds on men,
　　And death once dead, there's no more dying then.

My love is as a fever, longing still
For that which longer nurseth the disease,
Feeding on that which doth preserve the ill,
Th'uncertain sickly appetite to please.
My reason, the physician to my love,
Angry that his prescriptions are not kept,
Hath left me, and I desperate now approve
Desire is death, which physic did except.
Past cure I am, now reason is past care,
And frantic mad with evermore unrest.
My thoughts and my discourse as madmen's are,
At random from the truth vainly expressed;
   For I have sworn thee fair, and thought thee bright,
   Who art as black as hell, as dark as night.

O me, what eyes hath love put in my head,
Which have no correspondence with true sight!
Or if they have, where is my judgement fled,
That censures falsely what they see aright?
If that be fair whereon my false eyes dote,
What means the world to say it is not so?
If it be not, then love doth well denote
Love's eye is not so true as all men's. No,
How can it, O, how can love's eye be true,
That is so vexed with watching and with tears?
No marvel then though I mistake my view:
The sun itself sees not till heaven clears.
    O cunning love, with tears thou keep'st me blind
    Lest eyes, well seeing, thy foul faults should find!

Canst thou, O cruel, say I love thee not
When I against myself with thee partake?
Do I not think on thee when I forgot
Am of myself, all-tyrant, for thy sake?
Who hateth thee that I do call my friend?
On whom frown'st thou that I do fawn upon?
Nay, if thou lour'st on me, do I not spend
Revenge upon myself with present moan?
What merit do I in myself respect
That is so proud thy service to despise,
When all my best doth worship thy defect,
Commanded by the motion of thine eyes?
    But, love, hate on; for now I know thy mind.
    Those that can see thou lov'st, and I am blind.

O, from what power hast thou this powerful might
With insufficiency my heart to sway,
To make me give the lie to my true sight
And swear that brightness doth not grace the day?
Whence hast thou this becoming of things ill,
That in the very refuse of thy deeds
There is such strength and warrantise of skill
That in my mind thy worst all best exceeds?
Who taught thee how to make me love thee more
The more I hear and see just cause of hate?
O, though I love what others do abhor,
With others thou shouldst not abhor my state.
   If thy unworthiness raised love in me,
    More worthy I to be beloved of thee.

Love is too young to know what conscience is,
Yet who knows not conscience is born of love?
Then, gentle cheater, urge not my amiss,
Lest guilty of my faults thy sweet self prove.
For, thou betraying me, I do betray
My nobler part to my gross body's treason.
My soul doth tell my body that he may
Triumph in love; flesh stays no farther reason,
But rising at thy name doth point out thee
As his triumphant prize. Proud of this pride,
He is contented thy poor drudge to be,
To stand in thy affairs, fall by thy side.
    No want of conscience hold it that I call
    Her 'love' for whose dear love I rise and fall.

In loving thee thou know'st I am forsworn,
But thou art twice forsworn to me love swearing:
In act thy bed-vow broke, and new faith torn
In vowing new hate after new love bearing.
But why of two oaths' breach do I accuse thee
When I break twenty? I am perjured most,
For all my vows are oaths but to misuse thee,
And all my honest faith in thee is lost.
For I have sworn deep oaths of thy deep kindness,
Oaths of thy love, thy truth, thy constancy,
And to enlighten thee gave eyes to blindness,
Or made them swear against the thing they see.
 For I have sworn thee fair—more perjured eye
 To swear against the truth so foul a lie.

Cupid laid by his brand and fell asleep.
A maid of Dian's this advantage found,
And his love-kindling fire did quickly steep
In a cold valley-fountain of that ground,
Which borrowed from this holy fire of love
A dateless lively heat, still to endure,
And grew a seething bath which yet men prove
Against strange maladies a sovereign cure.
But at my mistress' eye love's brand new fired,
The boy for trial needs would touch my breast.
I, sick withal, the help of bath desired,
And thither hied, a sad distempered guest,
   But found no cure; the bath for my help lies
   Where Cupid got new fire: my mistress' eyes.

The little love-god lying once asleep
Laid by his side his heart-inflaming brand,
Whilst many nymphs that vowed chaste life to keep
Came tripping by; but in her maiden hand
The fairest votary took up that fire
Which many legions of true hearts had warmed,
And so the general of hot desire
Was sleeping by a virgin hand disarmed.
This brand she quenchèd in a cool well by,
Which from love's fire took heat perpetual,
Growing a bath and healthful remedy
For men diseased; but I, my mistress' thrall,
    Came there for cure; and this by that I prove:
    Love's fire heats water, water cools not love.

A
LOVER'S
COMPLAINT

From off a hill whose concave womb re-worded
A plaintful story from a sist'ring vale,
My spirits t'attend this double voice accorded,
And down I laid to list the sad-tuned tale;
Ere long espied a fickle maid full pale,
Tearing of papers, breaking rings a-twain,
Storming her world with sorrow's wind and rain.

Upon her head a plaited hive of straw
Which fortified her visage from the sun,
Whereon the thought might think sometime it saw
The carcass of a beauty spent and done.
Time had not scythèd all that youth begun,
Nor youth all quit; but spite of heaven's fell rage,
Some beauty peeped through lattice of seared age.

A LOVER'S COMPLAINT

Oft did she heave her napkin to her eyne,
Which on it had conceited characters,
Laund'ring the silken figures in the brine
That seasoned woe had pelleted in tears,
And often reading what contents it bears;
As often shrieking undistinguished woe
In clamours of all size, both high and low.

Sometimes her levelled eyes their carriage ride
As they did batt'ry to the spheres intend;
Sometime diverted their poor balls are tied
To th'orbèd earth; sometimes they do extend
Their view right on; anon their gazes lend
To every place at once, and nowhere fixed,
The mind and sight distractedly commixed.

Her hair, nor loose nor tied in formal plait,
Proclaimed in her a careless hand of pride;
For some, untucked, descended her sheaved hat,
Hanging her pale and pinèd cheek beside.
Some in her threaden fillet still did bide,
And, true to bondage, would not break from thence,
Though slackly braided in loose negligence.

A LOVER'S COMPLAINT

A thousand favours from a maund she drew
Of amber, crystal, and of beaded jet,
Which one by one she in a river threw
Upon whose weeping margin she was set;
Like usury applying wet to wet,
Or monarch's hands that lets not bounty fall
Where want cries some, but where excess begs all.

Of folded schedules had she many a one
Which she perused, sighed, tore, and gave the flood;
Cracked many a ring of posied gold and bone,
Bidding them find their sepulchres in mud;
Found yet more letters sadly penned in blood,
With sleided silk feat and affectedly
Enswathed and sealed to curious secrecy.

These often bathed she in her fluxive eyes,
And often kissed, and often 'gan to tear;
Cried 'O false blood, thou register of lies,
What unapprovèd witness dost thou bear!
Ink would have seemed more black and damnèd here!'
This said, in top of rage the lines she rents,
Big discontent so breaking their contents.

A reverend man that grazed his cattle nigh,
Sometime a blusterer that the ruffle knew
Of court, of city, and had let go by
The swiftest hours observèd as they flew,
Towards this afflicted fancy fastly drew,
And, privileged by age, desires to know
In brief the grounds and motives of her woe.

So slides he down upon his grainèd bat,
And comely distant sits he by her side,
When he again desires her, being sat,
Her grievance with his hearing to divide.
If that from him there may be aught applied
Which may her suffering ecstasy assuage,
'Tis promised in the charity of age.

'Father,' she says, 'though in me you behold
The injury of many a blasting hour,
Let it not tell your judgement I am old;
Not age, but sorrow over me hath power.
I might as yet have been a spreading flower,
Fresh to myself, if I had self-applied
Love to myself, and to no love beside.

'But, woe is me, too early I attended
A youthful suit—it was to gain my grace—
O, one by nature's outwards so commended
That maidens' eyes stuck over all his face.
Love lacked a dwelling and made him her place,
And when in his fair parts she did abide
She was new-lodged and newly deified.

'His browny locks did hang in crookèd curls,
And every light occasion of the wind
Upon his lips their silken parcels hurls.
What's sweet to do, to do will aptly find.
Each eye that saw him did enchant the mind,
For on his visage was in little drawn
What largeness thinks in paradise was sawn.

'Small show of man was yet upon his chin;
His phoenix down began but to appear,
Like unshorn velvet, on that termless skin
Whose bare outbragged the web it seemed to wear;
Yet showed his visage by that cost more dear,
And nice affections wavering stood in doubt
If best were as it was, or best without.

'His qualities were beauteous as his form,
For maiden-tongued he was, and thereof free.
Yet if men moved him, was he such a storm
As oft twixt May and April is to see
When winds breathe sweet, unruly though they be.
His rudeness so with his authorized youth
Did livery falseness in a pride of truth.

'Well could he ride, and often men would say
"That horse his mettle from his rider takes;
Proud of subjection, noble by the sway,
What rounds, what bounds, what course, what stop
        he makes!"
And controversy hence a question takes,
Whether the horse by him became his deed,
Or he his manège by th' well-doing steed.

'But quickly on this side the verdict went:
His real habitude gave life and grace
To appertainings and to ornament,
Accomplished in himself, not in his case.
All aids, themselves made fairer by their place,
Came for additions; yet their purposed trim
Pieced not his grace, but were all graced by him.

A LOVER'S COMPLAINT

'So on the tip of his subduing tongue
All kind of arguments and question deep,
All replication prompt, and reason strong,
For his advantage still did wake and sleep.
To make the weeper laugh, the laugher weep,
He had the dialect and different skill,
Catching all passions in his craft of will,

'That he did in the general bosom reign
Of young, of old, and sexes both enchanted,
To dwell with him in thoughts, or to remain
In personal duty, following where he haunted.
Consents bewitched, ere he desire, have granted,
And dialogued for him what he would say,
Asked their own wills, and made their wills obey.

'Many there were that did his picture get
To serve their eyes, and in it put their mind,
Like fools that in th'imagination set
The goodly objects which abroad they find
Of lands and mansions, theirs in thought assigned,
And labour in more pleasures to bestow them
Than the true gouty landlord which doth owe them.

'So many have, that never touched his hand,
Sweetly supposed them mistress of his heart.
My woeful self, that did in freedom stand,
And was my own fee-simple, not in part,
What with his art in youth, and youth in art,
Threw my affections in his charmèd power,
Reserved the stalk and gave him all my flower.

'Yet did I not, as some my equals did,
Demand of him, nor being desirèd yielded.
Finding myself in honour so forbid,
With safest distance I mine honour shielded.
Experience for me many bulwarks builded
Of proofs new bleeding, which remained the foil
Of this false jewel and his amorous spoil.

'But ah, who ever shunned by precedent
The destined ill she must herself assay,
Or forced examples 'gainst her own content
To put the by-past perils in her way?
Counsel may stop awhile what will not stay,
For when we rage, advice is often seen,
By blunting us, to make our wills more keen.

A LOVER'S COMPLAINT

'Nor gives it satisfaction to our blood
That we must curb it upon others' proof,
To be forbod the sweets that seems so good
For fear of harms that preach in our behoof.
O appetite, from judgement stand aloof!
The one a palate hath that needs will taste,
Though reason weep, and cry it is thy last.

'For further I could say this man's untrue,
And knew the patterns of his foul beguiling;
Heard where his plants in others' orchards grew,
Saw how deceits were gilded in his smiling,
Knew vows were ever brokers to defiling,
Thought characters and words merely but art,
And bastards of his foul adulterate heart.

'And long upon these terms I held my city
Till thus he gan besiege me: "Gentle maid,
Have of my suffering youth some feeling pity,
And be not of my holy vows afraid.
That's to ye sworn to none was ever said;
For feasts of love I have been called unto,
Till now did ne'er invite nor never woo.

' "All my offences that abroad you see
Are errors of the blood, none of the mind.
Love made them not; with acture they may be,
Where neither party is nor true nor kind.
They sought their shame that so their shame did find,
And so much less of shame in me remains
By how much of me their reproach contains.

' "Among the many that mine eyes have seen,
Not one whose flame my heart so much as warmèd
Or my affection put to th' smallest teen,
Or any of my leisures ever charmèd.
Harm have I done to them, but ne'er was harmèd;
Kept hearts in liveries, but mine own was free,
And reigned commanding in his monarchy.

' "Look here what tributes wounded fancies sent me
Of pallid pearls and rubies red as blood,
Figuring that they their passions likewise lent me
Of grief and blushes, aptly understood
In bloodless white and the encrimsoned mood—
Effects of terror and dear modesty,
Encamped in hearts, but fighting outwardly.

' "And lo, behold, these talents of their hair,
With twisted mettle amorously impleached,
I have received from many a several fair,
Their kind acceptance weepingly beseeched,
With th'annexations of fair gems enriched,
And deep-brained sonnets that did amplify
Each stone's dear nature, worth, and quality.

' "The diamond?—why, 'twas beautiful and hard,
Whereto his invised properties did tend;
The deep-green em'rald, in whose fresh regard
Weak sights their sickly radiance do amend;
The heaven-hued sapphire and the opal blend
With objects manifold; each several stone,
With wit well blazoned, smiled or made some moan.

' "Lo, all these trophies of affections hot,
Of pensived and subdued desires the tender,
Nature hath charged me that I hoard them not,
But yield them up where I myself must render—
That is to you, my origin and ender;
For these of force must your oblations be,
Since I their altar, you enpatron me.

' "O then advance of yours that phraseless hand
Whose white weighs down the airy scale of praise.
Take all these similes to your own command,
Hallowed with sighs that burning lungs did raise.
What me, your minister for you, obeys,
Works under you, and to your audit comes
Their distract parcels in combinèd sums.

' "Lo, this device was sent me from a nun,
A sister sanctified of holiest note,
Which late her noble suit in court did shun,
Whose rarest havings made the blossoms dote;
For she was sought by spirits of richest coat,
But kept cold distance, and did thence remove
To spend her living in eternal love.

' "But O, my sweet, what labour is't to leave
The thing we have not, mast'ring what not strives,
Planing the place which did no form receive,
Playing patient sports in unconstrainèd gyves!
She that her fame so to herself contrives
The scars of battle scapeth by the flight,
And makes her absence valiant, not her might.

' "O, pardon me, in that my boast is true!
The accident which brought me to her eye
Upon the moment did her force subdue,
And now she would the cagèd cloister fly.
Religious love put out religion's eye.
Not to be tempted would she be immured,
And now, to tempt, all liberty procured.

' "How mighty then you are, O hear me tell!
The broken bosoms that to me belong
Have emptied all their fountains in my well,
And mine I pour your ocean all among.
I strong o'er them, and you o'er me being strong,
Must for your victory us all congest,
As compound love to physic your cold breast.

' "My parts had power to charm a sacred nun,
Who disciplined, ay dieted in grace,
Believed her eyes when they t' assail begun,
All vows and consecrations giving place.
O most potential love, vow, bond, nor space
In thee hath neither sting, knot, nor confine,
For thou art all, and all things else are thine.

' "When thou impressest, what are precepts worth
Of stale example? When thou wilt inflame,
How coldly those impediments stand forth
Of wealth, of filial fear, law, kindred, fame.
Love's arms are peace, 'gainst rule, 'gainst sense,
    'gainst shame;
And sweetens in the suff'ring pangs it bears
The aloes of all forces, shocks, and fears.

' "Now all these hearts that do on mine depend,
Feeling it break, with bleeding groans they pine,
And supplicant their sighs to you extend
To leave the batt'ry that you make 'gainst mine,
Lending soft audience to my sweet design,
And credent soul to that strong bonded oath
That shall prefer and undertake my troth."

'This said, his wat'ry eyes he did dismount,
Whose sights till then were levelled on my face.
Each cheek a river running from a fount
With brinish current downward flowed apace.
O, how the channel to the stream gave grace,
Who glazed with crystal gate the glowing roses
That flame through water which their hue encloses.

A LOVER'S COMPLAINT

'O father, what a hell of witchcraft lies
In the small orb of one particular tear!
But with the inundation of the eyes
What rocky heart to water will not wear?
What breast so cold that is not warmèd here?
O cleft effect! Cold modesty, hot wrath,
Both fire from hence and chill extincture hath.

'For lo, his passion, but an art of craft,
Even there resolved my reason into tears.
There my white stole of chastity I daffed,
Shook off my sober guards and civil fears;
Appear to him as he to me appears,
All melting, though our drops this diff'rence bore:
His poisoned me, and mine did him restore.

'In him a plenitude of subtle matter,
Applied to cautels, all strange forms receives,
Of burning blushes or of weeping water,
Or swooning paleness; and he takes and leaves,
In either's aptness, as it best deceives,
To blush at speeches rank, to weep at woes,
Or to turn white and swoon at tragic shows,

'That not a heart which in his level came
Could scape the hail of his all-hurting aim,
Showing fair nature is both kind and tame,
And, veiled in them, did win whom he would maim.
Against the thing he sought he would exclaim;
When he most burned in heart-wished luxury,
He preached pure maid and praised cold chastity.

'Thus merely with the garment of a grace
The naked and concealèd fiend he covered,
That th'unexperient gave the tempter place,
Which like a cherubin above them hovered.
Who, young and simple, would not be so lovered?
Ay me, I fell, and yet do question make
What I should do again for such a sake.

'O that infected moisture of his eye,
O that false fire which in his cheek so glowed,
O that forced thunder from his heart did fly,
O that sad breath his spongy lungs bestowed,
O all that borrowed motion seeming owed
Would yet again betray the fore-betrayed,
And new pervert a reconcilèd maid.'

ALTERNATIVE VERSIONS OF SONNETS 2, 106, 138, AND 144

If, as there is good reason to believe, the 1609 edition of Shakespeare's Sonnets was printed from a transcript made by someone other than Shakespeare, it gives the poems at third-hand, at best. But a number of the sonnets survive in manuscript collections transcribed during the early seventeenth century which could have been copied from Shakespeare's own manuscript, and which in any case could represent the poems in genuinely Shakespearian versions different from those printed in 1609. The versions of Sonnets 2 and 106 printed below both derive from such manuscripts, and appear to represent the poems in either revised or unrevised form. The title of Sonnet 2, '*Spes Altera*', is a phrase from Virgil's *Aeneid*, Book XII, meaning 'a second hope'.

The versions of Sonnets 138 and 144 given below derive from *The Passionate Pilgrim*, an unauthorized volume of poems by Shakespeare and others ascribed wholly to Shakespeare and first printed in 1599. These too seem to represent the poems at a stage of composition different from that represented by the quarto.

'Spes Altera'

When forty winters shall besiege thy brow
And trench deep furrows in that lovely field,
Thy youth's fair liv'ry, so accounted now,
Shall be like rotten weeds of no worth held.
Then being asked where all thy beauty lies,
Where all the lustre of thy youthful days,
To say 'Within these hollow sunken eyes'
Were an all-eaten truth and worthless praise.
O how much better were thy beauty's use
If thou couldst say 'This pretty child of mine
Saves my account and makes my old excuse',
Making his beauty by succession thine.
   This were to be new born when thou art old,
   And see thy blood warm when thou feel'st it cold.

On his Mistress' Beauty

When in the annals of all-wasting time
I see descriptions of the fairest wights,
And beauty making beautiful old rhyme
In praise of ladies dead and lovely knights;
Then in the blazon of sweet beauty's best,
Of face, of hand, of lip, of eye, or brow,
I see their antique pen would have expressed
E'en such a beauty as you master now.
So all their praises were but prophecies
Of these our days, all you prefiguring,
And for they saw but with divining eyes
They had not skill enough your worth to sing;
    For we which now behold these present days
    Have eyes to wonder, but no tongues to praise.

When my love swears that she is made of truth
I do believe her though I know she lies,
That she might think me some untutored youth
Unskilful in the world's false forgeries.
Thus vainly thinking that she thinks me young,
Although I know my years be past the best,
I, smiling, credit her false-speaking tongue,
Outfacing faults in love with love's ill rest.
But wherefore says my love that she is young,
And wherefore say not I that I am old?
O, love's best habit's in a soothing tongue,
And age in love loves not to have years told.
    Therefore I'll lie with love, and love with me,
    Since that our faults in love thus smothered be.

Two loves I have, of comfort and despair,
That like two spirits do suggest me still.
My better angel is a man right fair,
My worser spirit a woman coloured ill.
To win me soon to hell my female evil
Tempteth my better angel from my side,
And would corrupt my saint to be a devil,
Wooing his purity with her fair pride;
And whether that my angel be turned fiend,
Suspect I may, yet not directly tell;
For being both to me, both to each friend,
I guess one angel in another's hell.
  The truth I shall not know, but live in doubt
  Till my bad angel fire my good one out.

TEXTUAL NOTES

The following substantive changes have been made to the 1609 edition; the original reading is given to the right of the bracket. Asterisked readings are original to this edition.

SONNETS

*12, l. 4   ensilvered o'er] or siluer'd ore
 13, l. 7   Yourself] You selfe
 17, l. 14 twice: in it] twise in it,
 23, l. 14 with . . . wit] wit . . . wiht
 24, l. 13 art:] art
 25, l. 9   might] worth
 26, l. 12 thy] their
 27, l. 10 thy] their
 28, l. 12 the even] th'eauen
 28, l. 14 strength] length
 31, l. 8   thee] there
 33, l. 11 alas] alack
 34, l. 12 cross] losse
 35, l. 8   thy . . . thy] their . . . their
 37, l. 7   thy] their
 39, l. 12 doth] dost
 43, l. 11 thy] their
 44, l. 12 attend] attend,
 44, l. 13 naught] naughts
 45, l. 11 assured] assured,
 45, l. 12 thy] their
 46, ll. 3, 8, 13, 14   thy] their
 47, l. 10 art] are
 47, l. 11 no] nor
*51, l. 11 rein] naigh
 55, l. 1   monuments] monument,
 56, l. 13 Or] As
 58, l. 7   patience, tame] patience tame,
 65, l. 12 of] or
 67, l. 6   seeming] seeing
 69, l. 3   due] end
 69, l. 5   Thy] Their

69, l. 14   soil] solye
70, l. 6   Thy] Their
73, l. 4   ruined] rn'wd
76, l. 7   tell] fel
77, l. 10   blanks] blacks
*82, l. 8   these] the
85, l. 3   thy] their
90, l. 11   shall] stall
91, l. 9   better] bitter
99, l. 4   dwells] dwells ?
99, l. 9   One] Our
102, l. 8   Her] his
106, l. 12   skill] still
111, l. 1   with] wish
113, l. 6   latch] lack
113, l. 13   more, replete] more repleat
113, l. 14   makes mine eye] maketh mine
117, l. 10   surmise accumulate] surmise, accumilate
118, l. 10   were not,] were, not
121, l. 11   bevel;] beuel
125, ll. 6–7   rent, . . . sweet] rent . . . sweet;
126, l. 8   minutes] mynuit
127, l. 10   brow] eyes
128, l. 3   sway'st] swayst,
128, l. 11   thy] their
128, l. 14   thy] their
129, l. 10   quest to have,] quest, to haue
129, l. 11   a] and
131, l. 9   swear,] sweare
132, l. 6   the east] th'East
137, l. 11   not,] not
138, l. 12   to have] t'haue
140, l. 13   belied] be lyde
144, l. 6   side] sight
146, l. 2   [   ]] My sinfull earth
153, l. 14   eyes] eye

TEXTUAL NOTES

A LOVER'S COMPLAINT

p. 169,	l. 16	'gan] gaue
p. 172,	l. 20	Came] Can
p. 173,	ll. 4–5	sleep.... weep,] sleep, ... weepe:
	l. 12	Consents] Consent's
	*l. 20	labour] labouring
p. 174,	l. 21	wills] wits
p. 175,	l. 21	woo] vovv
p. 177,	*l. 5	th'annexations] th'annexions
p. 178,	l. 5	me, your minister for you,] me your minister for you
	l. 9	A] Or
	*l. 18	Planing] Playing
p. 179,	l. 6	immured] enur'd
	l. 7	now, to tempt, all] now to tempt all
	l. 7	procured] procure
	l. 15	nun] Sunne
p. 180,	l. 4	kindred,] kindred
p. 181,	l. 6	O] Or

The Alternative Versions of Sonnets 2 and 106 are edited from a number of manuscript sources; of 138 and 144, from *The Passionate Pilgrim* (1599), with no substantive changes. The editor gratefully acknowledges textual assistance from Gary Taylor.

INDEX OF FIRST LINES
OF THE SONNETS

The references are to Sonnet numbers

INDEX OF FIRST LINES

INDEX OF FIRST LINES

INDEX OF FIRST LINES

INDEX OF FIRST LINES

INDEX OF FIRST LINES